A Journey to Inner Peace and Joy

Tracing Contemporary Chinese Hermits

A Journey to Inner Peace and Joy

Tracing Contemporary Chinese Hermits

ZHANG JIANFENG
TRANSLATED BY TONY BLISHEN

Better Link Press

Contents

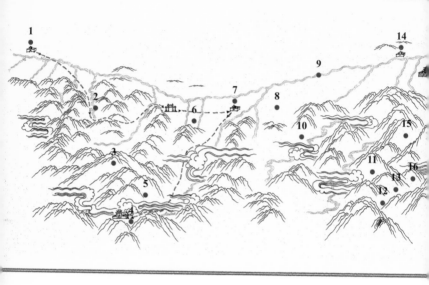

1	● Baoji municipality		8	● Caotang Temple
2	● Pan River valley		9	● Wei River
3	● Mount Taibai		10	● Ziwu valley
4	● Tiejiashu (Armor Tree) Temple		11	● Qingcha
5	● Houzhenzi		12	● Shibianyu
6	● Zhongnanzhen town		13	● Xianrencha
7	● County of Zhouzhi		14	● Xianyang

▲ Map of the Southern Hills. (*Drawing by Wang Xiaofei*)

Foreword

A Hermit Mountain
beneath the Moon

If you cross the Wei river and travel south past fields of growing wheat, maize and rice paddy it is easy to find steep narrow valleys filled with dandelion and bracken, polygonum and the *lingzhi* fungus. Birds call to each other, the clarity of their sound travelling from one valley to the next, they are sharing the joy in their hearts.

Sometimes, here and there, a wisp of blue cooking smoke drifts upwards, a few thatched huts below, a chrysanthemum fence, and by a window of bamboo, some copies of the classics. A hermit sits on a rock by the spring water or beneath the pines, smiling at the changing colors of the hills as clouds furl above spring water as green as the pine needles themselves ...

In the Southern Hills (Zhongnanshan), since time immemorial, this kind of scene has never been affected by external events. Many people come here from a distance and once in the hills one learns to be still. Going into the hills conserves one's in-born nature, the call of a few birds, a breath of mountain breeze and human language is then superfluous. There is no need for the *qin*, the mountain mists have their own music. The daoists said that a man was deaf if he could only hear the sound of thunder, and blind if he could only see bright colors. In the hills we can find ourselves and find our innate nature. There are very few ranges of hills that have

9

▲ A view of the Southern Hills (Photo/Guo Feng)

the majesty, the extent, the capacity and the mystery of the Southern Hills. Because of the virtue inherent in these hills, those who choose to become hermits there feel its existence as soon as they come close. As I have stood under the pines in these steep valleys I have often felt intoxicated, not knowing whether I was in a dream or in reality. In the eyes of some, the rocks of the Southern Hills are like so many pages of the classics, waiting for somebody with affinity to come and read them ...

The Southern Hills lie to the south of Xi'an in Shaanxi province. There is an ancient saying in China, "May your good fortune resemble the flowing waters of the Eastern Sea; may you live as long as the everlasting pines of the Southern Hills." Originally, a species of everlasting pine grew in the Southern Hills. The wood of these trees was loose grained, the branches were nothing but holes. It was no good for building nor was it any good as firewood, it just smoked without flame and woodcutters never chose them for felling. It took several hundred years for the everlasting pine to grow into a small tree and it only flowered once in several decades. They are the longest living trees to have been so far discovered in the world. Perhaps it was from these trees that the early daoists, practicing deep in the hills, first learned the secrets of longevity.

Over 60 years ago, a practitioner saw a cave on a cliff

in one of these gorges with a hermit sitting outside taking the sun. There was no track up the precipitous slope and he realized that whoever lived in the cave was no normal being. He asked the hermit's permission to look in the cave and the old man asked him several questions, the practitioner lowered his head deep in thought and when he looked up discovered that the cave was no longer there and that in its place was a single pine tree.

The buddhist monk Rucheng of the Wolong Temple said that many years ago one of the villagers had seen an elderly white haired, white-whiskered old monk standing at the side of the road that wound its way round the bottom of the hill gazing at the vehicles driving to and fro. The monk had asked him, what were they, these things on the road that rushed past so quickly? The villager told him that they were motor vehicles. The monk listened and then turned on his heel and went back up into the hills.

Many years ago an ancient descended from the hills with a sack of walnuts slung over his back to exchange for cloth with the locals, his clothing was so ragged that at best it could only form a skirt. Out of curiosity, the villagers asked him how many years he had lived in the hills. The old man replied that he didn't know how long he had lived there. He lived in a cave and had converted two black bears as disciples and during the winter he passed the days with a bear snuggled up to him on either side.

When we reached the Jintaiguan temple the legend there was that the Ming dynasty hermit Zhang Sanfeng had left an empty bowl after eating that had been there for 500 years. He had never returned and it was said that he had later appeared elsewhere in the hills. I always believed that he had travelled away on a cloud and that we had merely brushed shoulders with him in passing and perhaps, if we were patient, he would return in a while.

In front of the tomb of Laozi we came across several old men discussing the Way. One old hermit said that the Way that present-day society followed was the Way of commerce, people were no longer willing to practice the great Way. He directed us to another hermit upon whom to call. That hermit asked me what questions I had. He said self cultivation was a lifetime's occupation, he was old and it was not easy for him to talk, he was striving to turn himself into a vessel for the Way, only then could it be sustained. This required a lengthy process. He had been there many years, all he had done was to try to calm himself, so that the troubles of the external world could no longer disturb him, nor had he created trouble himself, that was all. The Way I sought was within myself, that was starting point of our roaming, and that was where we had to return finally before we could clearly perceive the true nature of the world.

I met a peasant up in the hills and talked about hermits with him. He said that if you looked at the cool breezes in the hills they seemed hidden but weren't hidden, they were just there. Where was the ultimate hermit? Even if we became invisible it would be impossible to completely sever spiritual contact with the outside world, hidden and not hidden were like night and day, all as free as the passing clouds and flowing water. There were some people who lived in seclusion amongst the forests and streams and never set foot in a town, they abandoned the world of dust and approached the absolutes of life directly. There are people who say that there have never really been any true hermits, those who have been sighted and are called hermits were merely thinking about being hermits. A recluse said that being a hermit was if I stood in front of you and you would never know who I was. Nan Huaijin (1918-2012), scholar of Chinese civilization and culture, said in *Zhuangzi Nanhua*, his commentary on the daoist philosopher Zhuangzi: "From ancient times it has been impossible to know accurately about the deeds of genuine hermits, they are just those who the daoists have either collected or faked into the obscure biographies of the immortals."

In the long, several thousand year history of China, it was only the talented and learned who, though they possessed the ability to become officials, did not do so and did not make the effort to do so, who were known under the title of "hermit". They advocated an attitude to life based on nature and inaction and chose a lifestyle of self cultivation that shunned the world. Today the community of hermits is more extensive. They may be scholars or peasants, petty traders, daoists, or buddhist monks. They do not suffer the interference of the times nor are they trammeled by the secular world and they are remote from the clamor of world of dust. They are content in poverty and take joy in spirituality. They cherish an unrevealed treasure and winnow pure wisdom from coarse straw.

In the '80s of the last century the American sinologist Bill Porter travelled deep into the Southern Hills in search of hermits and found practitioners of many religions. In the introduction to the Chinese edition of his book he wrote: "The reason for writing this book is this. I want the practitioners of all religions in the West to know that despite China's history of

13

war and revolution, practitioners of religion still persevere, I hope thereby to encourage western practitioners."

I came across Bill Porter's *Road to Heaven* several years ago and was greatly encouraged to travel alone deep into the Southern Hills south of Xi'an in search of hermits. Because I did not know where exactly in the hills the hermits were I followed the routes used by the countless hermits of the past. I started my search from Nanwutai to the south of Xi'an and followed the mountain valley westwards to distant Ziwuyu and then penetrated as far as Dayu and Huashan at the eastern end of Nanwutai and then on to Taibaishan and further west where I completed my search.

In fact, Bill Porter's search was conducted over twenty years ago and since then there have been great changes in China. People who have aspired to the practice of Daoism have left their temples and have gone into the hills where they practice in silent meditation. At the same time, economic development has caused people to harbor higher spiritual aspirations and to begin to reassess some aspects of society. Some writers, poets and artists have begun to try a life different from that of the city and to seek a spiritual home. Others, enlightened by Chinese traditional culture and their conscious demands upon it have begun to take to the hills for the cultivation of self and spirit. They differ from the ancient hermit masters. The scope of the Chinese hermit today is much broader, for the most part they seek inner calm and spiritual detachment.

The people I sought who lived secluded in the hills had one thing in common—a genuine simplicity combined with a lack of interest in wealth and fame, they may have been haggard in appearance but they possessed peace of mind. They

◀ A hermit on Mount Huashan (Photo/Zhang Jianfeng)

were making a conscious return to their original state, they were at one with nature and communed with beasts and birds. Their relationships with one another were comfortable and simple, they maintained an ancient morality, living in wisdom and tranquility. This was the life that the people of China had sought and esteemed for thousands of years. It is my journey of discovery into this garden of the other world that I want to share with my readers.

Chapter One

The Hidden Man and the Everlasting Way

Nan Huaijin, the well known scholar of Chinese civilization described the importance of hermits in Chinese culture thus: "Historically speaking, hermetic ideas have occupied the most sublime and most important positions within the spirit of Chinese culture, it is merely that rather like the form of the hermits themselves, they always adopted methods that were private, unknown to the world but satisfying to the self. Thus, they are easily overlooked and easily forgotten. To put it more emphatically, hermetic thought and historic hermits themselves have actually been the behind-the-scenes operators of Chinese culture."

For a long time in China's past, the practice of asceticism was the fundamental of the hermetic life. In the biographical *Standard History of the Later Han (Hou Han Shu)* which covers the years 25 – 220 AD, there is a passage describing hermits: "Some live in seclusion to achieve their aspirations, some are hidden away to complete the Way, some calm themselves to suppress their ill humor, some take to the heights to seek peace, some regard the vulgar life as filth, some seek to develop purity through finding and eradicating fault."

Later, the term hermit applied to those with the ability to become an official but who did not do so and did not make the effort to do so. To the Chinese, being a hermit means a

▲ The hermits path to the Southern Hills

detachment from the common world as well as the possession of a wisdom and ability that is almost unattainable for the ordinary person. Over the several thousand years of Chinese history it has been those ethereal beings the hermits who have won the envy and respect of the populace. They chose the hermetic life not because of the demands of society but because of a need to look into their own lives.

The day-to-day working philosophy of the hermits was to manifest the natural strength of the heavenly law through a form of soft power and to make the strength of mankind yield to the strength of nature, to abandon fame and riches, to maintain morality and personal integrity and to live in poverty with dignity.

Originally, the single character道(dao) represented the

whole of Chinese philosophy. However, 2,000 years ago it was split into two camps, Daoism and Confucianism. The Confucians exerted their utmost to strive for the attainment of universal government, rose in the ranks at court and were therefore sometimes corrupted by the mundane world. The daoists embraced nature and the Way and looked on fame and wealth as floods or wild animals, they feared lest the contamination of the dust of the mundane world should soil their garments. Nevertheless, they never took their eyes off world of dust, when the world was in uproar they made a timely appearance from the hills and rebuilt social order on the basis of the heavenly law and the will of the people, afterwards retreating back to the tranquility of the hills.

Nan Huaijin said: "When we come to talk of daoist thought, it cannot be separated from the thinking of the hermits. Rather than say that the origins of Daoism lie in the Yellow Emperor and Laozi, or in Laozi and Zhuangzi, it would be more appropriate to say that the origin of Daoism lies with the hermits and that it then evolved into the ideas of Laozi and Zhuangzi, or of the Yellow Emperor and Laozi."

The philosopher Laozi (c.571 – 471 BC) is well known in the West. His wisdom has been summarized as purity and inaction. Purity and inaction means distance from desire, only through the absence of excessive desire can there be the wisdom to see all living things clearly.

Because Laozi was a hermit, scholars have been debating the twisted skeins of his life for several thousand years without reaching any definite hypothesis. The mainstream theory is that Laozi was born in the area of present day Henan province and was an official under the Zhou dynasty. In the final years of the dynasty he recognized its impending collapse and mounted a young ox and made his way westwards to the Hangu Pass. The official at the Hangu Pass was a practitioner called Yin Xi, who, before he held the post at Hangu and because of his skill in astronomy and weather forecasting, had been dispatched by the Zhou emperor to the Southern Hills to observe the stars. He was aware of Laozi's imminent arrival through his forecasting skills and took him aside when he arrived at the pass. He welcomed Laozi to a thatched hut in the west of the Southern Hills where Laozi expounded the *Classic of Morality* (*Daodejing*) to him. After leaving behind the *Classic of Morality*, Laozi floated away in the air no one knows whither.

Zhuangzi (c. 369 – 286 BC), a loyal follower of Laozi, is another important hermit in the history of Chinese culture. Zhuangzi's ancestors came from the nobility of the state of Chu. He spent his life as a minor official in charge of the lacquer plantations and for much of the time poverty made his life difficult to sustain and he was obliged to plait straw sandals in return for rice. King Wei of Chu heard of his reputation and dispatched an emissary to offer him a position at court, which he refused. He believed that being an official harmed man's basic nature and that it was better to live in poverty happily. He likened himself to a turtle crawling clumsily in the mud, although it was difficult it allowed more time for concern for the world and for oneself.

Zhuangzi held that everything in the universe, living or otherwise, was equal in nature. Man was absorbed into these universal phenomena and thus began and ended with the universe. He advocated fostering the dominant factor in life, that is to say the spirit and valued the cultivation of inner virtue. In his eyes, adequacy of virtue would give rise to a self sufficient spiritual strength. He promoted the idea of following the laws of nature and of taking things as they come in an attempt to arrive at a carefree state where success could be achieved without having to rely on external strength.

It is said that Zhuangzi was so dissatisfied with the lack of

▲ The author in the hills with a practitioner (Photo/Guo Feng)

tranquility at the lacquer plantation that he became a hermit in the Southern Hills. He reduced his desires and material needs to the minimum believing that only the theory of inaction could ensure survival. The diversity of all living things was born of inaction, so that it would be enough just to protect the fundamental root from which all physical phenomena sprang.

Kongzi (Confucius) (551 – 479 BC) who was contemporary with Laozi and Zhuangzi, inherited the Way from previous generations but what he sought was to persuade the monarchs who held power to comply with morality and to return to it and to develop a social system, based on the laws of morality, that conformed with human nature. To this end he was indefatigable and throughout his life took to the road to spread this word amongst the various states. He had once sought instruction on the Way from Laozi who had criticized him for having too many ideas. Laozi had warned the deeply

▲ Practitioners in a cave (Photo/Zhang Jianfeng)

anxious Kongzi:

"Heaven and Earth proceed by themselves unmoved by man, the Sun and the Moon shine of themselves without being lit by man, the stars order themselves without being arranged by man, birds and beasts exist without being created by man, this is as nature made it, why should it require the labor of man? Man lives and dies, is honored and is disgraced, all through the laws and way of nature. Follow the laws of nature, respect the way of nature and states will order themselves and man will correct himself. What need is there for an effusion of rites and music and the preaching of humanity and righteousness? Such an effusion of rites and music and the preaching of humanity and righteousness is far from man's nature! It is like banging a drum in pursuit of one who has escaped, the louder it sounds the further he escapes!"

Laozi's criticism in no way diminished Kongzi's enthusiasm for the implementation of politics. Kongzi subsequently came across a number of hermits on his travels, one of them was Jieyu, the madman of Chu, whose criticism of Kongzi was even fiercer. Jieyu met Kongzi's carriage singing: "Phoenix! Oh, Phoenix! Why so downcast on this day of virtuous fate? The past is beyond repair but the future gives time to repent. Enough! Enough! Those in power are in peril!" Wishing to speak with him, Kongzi dismounted but to his great regret Jieyu made off.

Unlike daoist hermits, those hermits who had been deeply influenced by the theories of the Confucian school always placed greater emphasis upon a high minded but not excessive wisdom. They were familiar with the *Book of Songs* and *The Book of History* and with ceremony and music and admired the customs of the past, they valued personal conduct and integrity above their own lives.

The distinguished rulers at court and the hermits and worthies secluded amongst the rivers and lakes were continually pushing Chinese history forward. At the point where the Confucian intellectuals, whose self imposed role was to help the world, encountered insurmountable political problems or when politics themselves became corrupt, the hermits hidden away up in the hills began, in their own way, to play an indirect part in society. They either dispatched their own disciples to take office or became advisers to the monarch, though they may have been located in the hills their gaze never left the mundane world of dust.

Zhuge Liang can be called the most famous hermit in Chinese history. During the period of the Three Kingdoms (220 – 280) at a time of internecine warfare Liu Bei, a descendent of the Han royal house, harbored designs upon the whole state but because those close to him lacked genius he was obliged to content himself with a corner of the territory, even at times having no space of his own and having to seek shelter with others. While Liu Bei was searching far and wide for a worthy to consult he came across the hermit Sima Hui, aloof from the world and as free as a bird. Sima Hui recommended one of his students Zhuge Liang. At the time, Zhuge Liang had been a hermit at Nanyang for ten years, tilling the fields and studying the world, filled with ideas of strategy. Liu Bei visited Zhuge Liang's thatched hut three times and finally succeeded in meeting him. In order to repay Liu Bei's patronage Zhuge Liang gave up the hermetic life and accompanied Liu Bei on his military campaigns.

Zhuge Liang undertook innumerable campaigns during his lifetime. He was legendary for his mysterious ability to assess situations and for his profound insight. He was often able to understand the situation of the enemy forces through his use of daoist methods of forecasting and was skilled in deploying troops on the basis of occult formulas derived from the *Book of Changes* (*Yi Jing*), thereby seizing the initiative on the battlefield. On one occasion he repelled an army of tens of thousands merely by sitting atop an empty battlement playing the *qin*.

Zhuge Liang helped Liu Bei to establish the Shu-Han regime as equal in power to the states of Wu and Wei and occupying a third of the territory of China. Liu Bei also entrusted him with the task of placing his successor, Liu Chan, on the imperial throne. Zhuge Liang finally died of exhaustion on active service. Not long after his death the Shu-Han regime was annexed by the state of Wei.

During his lifetime, Zhuge Liang called on the next generation to express ambition through simplicity of life and to

▶ A daoist master at practice in the Southern Hills (Photo/Zhang Jianfeng)

achieve through tranquility. Zhuge Liang, when chief minister of the state of Shu, took a woman famed for her ugliness as his wife and together they invented the wheel barrow. In the end however, he only left his descendants a homestead of about five *mou* (just under an acre) and some mulberry trees, the land for tilling and the mulberry trees for raising silkworms. Throughout his life he advocated tilling the fields and study as an aid to self cultivation.

In the eyes of the Chinese, Zhuge Liang has always been the incarnation of wisdom, like a mysterious star twinkling in the heavens earning the respect of people's hearts. Many Chinese of great wisdom were hermits by nature. If a man wishes to shine brilliantly in life he must build up his power. Whether expressed through a daoist nature or in the theories of Confucianism, the hermits always gained a broader space by withdrawing to cultivate mind and spirit.

For several thousand years the Chinese have encouraged and admired true hermits, irrespective of whether a person becomes a hermit because of the Way, or just to seek tranquility, a retreat to a life of tranquility in the hills will always one day lead him to the embrace of the Way.

Chapter Two

Nanwutai
—A Humble Door to the Southern Hills

For most people, the first step towards the Southern Hills is taken at Nanwutai. I had already been to the face of the mountain, which was crowded by tourists and where there were several monasteries. Prior to the 50s of the 20th century, several hundred monasteries of various sizes had extended from the top of the front of the mountain to its foot. Nowadays, the largest is called Zizhulin, the Black Bamboo Forest, and at the foot of the mountain there are the Shengshou and Mituo temples. Since the front of the mountain faces the red dust of the world that lies at its foot, it tends to be rather noisy. An old man stands at the top selling walking sticks and many people who pass him increase their possessions by the addition of a black bamboo walking stick.

The path extends towards the rear slope of the mountain. To the east is Qingliangtai the highest peak of Nanwutai, further east still is Guanyintai, from where you can see the western peak of Mount Cuihuashan; less than 200 meters down the southern slope is Great Maopeng (Great Hut, later known as the Xilin temple), with its huge closed doors, concealed on a precipice on the rear slope of Nanwutai, facing the mountain ranges that stretch away southwards. In their time, Masters Xuyun (1840 – 1959), Laiguo (1881 – 1953), and Yinguang (1861 – 1940) were all installed here; like mushrooms after

rain, the thatched huts of hermits sprouted everywhere in the dense forest and under the cliffs of the rear slope of Nanwutai. This is hermit paradise.

Little Maopeng (Little Hut) lies about the distance of a meal from Great Maopeng. On several occasions I have encountered a hermit loaded with food making the round trip between the two Maopengs. For a long time in the past, Little Maopeng was almost a sister to Great Maopeng.

The entrance to Little Maopeng was concealed amidst flowering trees and there is a large tall rock beneath the piled stones of the main entrance. As we stood at the gate, I was transfixed. There was a bird's nest at the top of a tree by the gate from which a pica bird was singing. Under the noonday sun of an April day, the flower blossomed like a market but the scent of the undergrowth reached the nostrils first. I had passed through here twice before, either in the summer or in the autumn and apart from hearing the barking of dogs I had seen nothing. Armed with a little experience of visiting Maopeng, I recited the name of the Amitabha Buddha and knocked on the wooden door.

A lay buddhist soon came to open the door, we explained our purpose and she pulled back the dog and let us into the courtyard. The master of Maopeng was away and the lay sister was looking after the place. Two nuns, Chengbo and Miaoyue lived here, they had gone to Pushan Maopeng (the Hut of Universal Virtue) at Xionggou (Bear's Gully), sister house to Little Maopeng.

Behind the building at Little Maopeng was a large rock with a spring beneath it which the lay caretaker took us to see. The water from the spring was so clear that it was almost impossible to see that it existed, but its refreshing coolness

◀ Nanwutai (Photo/Zhang Jianfeng)

raised our spirits, it was the drinking water for Little Maopeng. Yang Xiaobing, the photographer who accompanied us saw the water and started to complain that he hadn't been able to bring tea-making utensils into the hills to make tea here. On the window sill was a kitchen slice that had been almost worn away. The caretaker said that it had once been used by the master's master, someone had given them a new one before they arrived and this one was now used to gather vegetables.

The American Bill Porter penned a description of Chengbo's master, the nun Huiyuan and her apple tree. The apple tree is still there but Mother Huiyuan has died and her stupa stands below the courtyard at Maopeng.

To stop the dog barking at us the caretaker quickly covered its eyes with her hand. We skirted round it and saw Mother Huiyuan's stupa where golden yellow bees hummed busily amongst the flowers and the rocks were covered with shining green moss.

The path finished close to a steep valley where a patch of abandoned grass lay before us, in its depths there was an overgrown thatched hut with a stone terrace in front and a thicket of bamboo below. A monk stood on the terrace holding a copy of one of the sutras, this scene caught us by pleasant surprise. Without thinking I raised my camera to take a photograph but the monk appeared startled and made off. He refused to be photographed but was willing to converse.

There were three mud huts whose period of building could be distinguished. Written on the mud wall beneath the eaves were the two words: cease speech. This practitioner had planted a strip of cabbages which grew enticingly, as if just waiting to be stolen. I asked the hermit the name of the thatched huts in front

▶ The mountain gate to Little Maopeng (Little Hut) on the rear slope of Nanwutai (Photo/Zhang Jianfeng)

of us, he said that they did not need a name.

Q: How do you normally practice Buddhism?

A: I read this (showing me the sutra he was holding in his hand), the Buddha expounded for nine years on the single character *miao* (wonderful).

Q: Is there anybody here in the hills who has achieved enlightenment?

A: They practice for a certain amount of time and then leave, they can't stay, there are too many people in the hills. Those who have achieved some cultivation intensely dislike being disturbed, those with a little cultivation are pursued for financial support. They didn't come and live here in order to be supported by others, so they escape far away.

Q: What's your life like normally?

A: My life is very simple, I live here. As long as one has the right mindset, even grass can be appetizing. Cattle eat grass but are always fat. What you eat is not important.

We clasped our hands in greeting, said goodbye to the mountain monk and went on our way.

The path had reached the bottom of the ravine and we followed the course of a small stream out of it. The first thatched hut that we came across in the ravine was a nameless hut under construction whose occupant was the nun Mother Honghui. She was working alongside the builders on the site, working next to her was a young man as clean-cut as a bamboo shoot. He told us that this valley was called Xionggou (Bear's Gully). He said it was not wise to travel here after dark because of black bears. We guessed that he might be her brother, they both looked alike.

The hut would soon be finished and had five rooms, all that was left was the roof. Mother Honghui invited us to attend the consecration when it was finished.

We walked on past the Qingjing Maopeng (the Tranquil Hut), there should have been another hut, the year before there had been a hut on an abandoned mill-stone beside the road. A three roomed hut with vegetables growing beside it in which two monks had been living. The roadside had been dense with persimmon trees, their leaves had fallen, nobody had picked the persimmons and they had dropped to the ground, staining the stones red. We had seen the occupants of the hut beside a stone bridge over the stream. They were gathering herbs, we didn't talk to them but greeted them from a distance and passed on our way.

There was a line of huts on the hill opposite to which Mother Honghui had given us directions, we had passed through here twice previously and had not discovered them. We were now in the second month of spring, the color of the grass had not deepened and the leaves on the trees were not yet out so that it was possible to make out the huts on the hill and the shapes of people. Amongst them was a hut called Lianchi Maopeng (the Lotus Pool Straw Hut), I secretly determined that next time, I would sit in rapt absorption at the entrance to that hut.

Once past the hut being built for Mother Honghui, the valley began to broaden out. At the entrance to the valley stood Pushan Maopeng built of red brick and consisting of three large halls, two dormitories for monks and a refectory. We sat by a table in the courtyard, this was the other bodhimanda or place of enlightenment of Mother Chengbo, the occupant of Little Maopeng, who many years ago when she was young had followed her master and lived in the hills. She was now over fifty years of age.

There were three lay buddhists in the courtyard, one of them, fifty or more years old, was a peasant woman from a neighboring village who would not admit to being a lay buddhist and said only that she came to help with the cooking.

Mother Miaoyue emerged from the building shortly and when she learned that we had come to visit specially she cheerfully organized the lay people into bringing us wheat buns and pickles and cooking spinach soup for us.

Mother Chengbo was not there and Mother Miaoyue was not much given to talking so we addressed ourselves to the wheat buns in the basket and drank up a large bowl of spinach soup.

After supper, Yang Xiaobing the photographer with us suggested taking Mother Miaoyue's photograph. After taking several photographs, he wanted to take a group photograph of Mother Miaoyue together with the lay buddhists but the peasant woman came rushing over in a fit of shyness, saying that she was not fit to have her photograph taken with the Mother, the lay people almost kidnapped her and placed her beside Mother Miaoyue.

To reach the valley we had to go through a village called Guanmiao. Alongside the village was a river and a path set with wild flowers, the track led to towards a number of huts deep in the valley and alongside it there was a tumbledown hotel and small shops.

We were almost through the village when a dog suddenly leaped out from somebody's courtyard as if it were about to tear us to pieces. Just then a peasant woman holding a rice bowl calmly appeared and quietly checked its attack. There were fields behind the village where peasants and oxen were laboriously engaged in cultivation. Chickens walked about amongst the wild chrysanthemums, evening cooking smoke drifted up from the village and sometimes the chickens suddenly took it into their heads to fly up and sleep in the trees.

I visited Xionggou once more after the rainy season between spring and summer. Mother Chengbo the abbess of Pushan Maopeng was attending a major buddhist ceremony of charity at the Xingjiao Temple off the mountain. I passed on with a sigh. The track twisted on by a stream that was stained green and white clouds blown from the distance billowed above the mountain peaks.

Several peasants were busy in the hills under the white clouds, Mother Honghui's hut now had a roof and the hut's chimney could be seen.

We looked at this brand new hut and were told that Mother Honghui was also off the mountain attending the ceremony, I was really dejected. The hut that was nearly finished was to be the future lower court of Qingjing Maopeng. Above its entrance was a 14 character incantation, smaller characters by its side explained that the act of passing under the incantation would eradicate all sin, consequently I passed in and out under the incantation to try and rid myself of sin. A moment later a large yellow dog bounded up followed immediately by the appearance of Mother Honghui's younger brother, his appearance giving assurance as to the whereabouts of lunch.

Hearing that we had come to see Mother Honghui he arranged for one of the peasant women on the site, the most skilled in rolling noodles, to go up to Qingjing Maopeng and make lunch for us. I immediately followed her up along a path through swaying wild flowers.

There were five rooms in Qingjing Maopeng and vegetables were planted in the courtyard to which there was a rear entrance. Behind the building there was a wood stack and a patch of bamboo. Water was piped up from an underground stream beneath the courtyard and as the water from the spring flowed out beside them the bamboos stirred in the wind. There was an intimacy between the bamboos and the spring water, they were both performing, during the day their audience was the white clouds, at night it was the moon and stars.

The inscription on the board at Qingjing Maopeng was by

Master Kuanji. Mother Honghui's younger brother told us that he was her master, he had gone off mountain as well.

Lay brother Kuankui, the younger brother, was the foreman at Qingjing Maopeng. The whole family were buddhists and before becoming a lay buddhist, Kuankui had been a businessman. When his elder sister had become a pupil of Master Kuanji she had supported him financially for over ten years. Several years ago she had taken a buddhist vow and become a real monk. The lay buddhists in the family had discussed it and determined that they would do everything in their power to build a hut for Honghui.

I asked lay brother Kuankui how a hut, a *maopeng* was put up. He said that there was another buddhist master who wanted to build a hut as a place for practice and enlightenment on this hill but so far only Mother Honghui's hut had been completed. That had gone smoothly and he was lucky that nobody had been injured in the process of construction. They had been fined 2,000 yuan by the forest conservation team at Shanya because they had felled the roof beams for the hut without a permit. That apart, he felt everything else had gone smoothly. Because he knew the area well the land had cost nothing and he had found hill dwellers to carry the bricks up on their backs for fifty cents a brick, the tiled five room hut had cost nearly 100,000 yuan. The family was not rich, in a town off the mountain good business could be done for that amount of money.

There were not many cultivators amongst the hill folk, much of the land was abandoned and overgrown. There were two households on the hill opposite who said that wild pig uprooted their crops and planting fruit trees was impossible because bears and other animals generally carried off the best fruit. The hill folk relied on building huts for the surrounding buddhist masters and doing casual jobs to earn money for food. Amongst them were the village chief and his relatives and the forest conservation team leader and his relatives. Apart from wages there was an extra meal at midday. Sometimes the children and old people joined the construction team. The hill folk brought their dogs to meals, so the dogs could enjoy a meal as well.

Mother Honghui had not had any financial support in her early days as a hermit and some people felt that her practice regime was rather heavy. I had once come across a monk climbing up the mountain path with a sack of flour on his back. He was very old but had to carry up on his back everything he needed for life in the hills.

Kuankui talked about the practitioners in the surrounding area. Several years previously there had been an ascetic monk in the valley. He had nowhere to live and worked for others every day fetching water, chopping wood, he had chopped firewood for many of the huts in the area, it was stacked at the back to the height of a man, he had chopped all the firewood in the those sturdy wood stacks. He only eat left-overs. The hut on the hill opposite was Lianchi Maopeng, occupied by Kuanfa, a fellow student of the same sect as Kuankui, their common master was Master Monk Changming, a 91 year old from the Xingjiao temple. Several years earlier when Kuanfa had just arrived in the hills he had wandered over half the mountain without any fixed destination, sometimes living in caves, there were bears at night in this valley. In the winter the mountains were sealed in by snow and there was little trace of humans. They rose at five and recited the sutras as they circled the building.

Kuanfa now had a fixed abode. It was said that his hut was well constructed and although built on a mountain ridge, it had a well equipped toilet and washing facilities. Up to the present, Kuanfa never eat after midday, he meditated in the

▲ Snow on Nanwutai (Photo/Tian Cuoshi)

sitting position all night and normally lived off mountain, coming up at weekends. His hut was on a ridge wreathed in clouds, facing south, where the earliest sun could be seen in the morning and the stars could be seen at night.

I visited the valley again the day after the great earthquake. Yellow shadows flitted past alongside the path, they were deer which had fled into the thick forest from the stream valleys beside the path. I easily found the familiar path hidden by weeds and walked up to the entrance to Qingjing Maopeng.

Kuanji, the occupant of Qingjing Maopeng was not away. He did not look in the least old and his face had an extraordinary radiance. He had a bad cough as a result of spending years living in a damp clay built building. He had been a monk for over 20 years and had previously been a practitioner of Chinese medicine. His master was also Master Monk Changming, abbot of the Xingjiao temple. I asked him about his practice of Buddhism in the hills, he smiled and gave a reply which shocked me—I work to earn my food. Life in the hills is very simple, chopping firewood and cooking, reciting the scriptures and sleeping. There are buddhist services off mountain that have to be attended, normally I live on the mountain.

Kuanji told me that our lives are made up from a combination of prime causes, daoists call them the elements of metal, wood, water, fire, and earth and buddhists call them the elements of earth, water, fire, air and void. For example, in cooking, wood has to be burned and wood produces fire, water is used and so is a stove of earth, all are contained within the five elements and within buddhist teaching.

As to practice, Master Kuanji believed that effort should not be excessive but that neither should one be lazy, the middle way was the best. It was a lengthy process and haste easily gave rise to problems.

In Master Kuanji's life, practice resembled the rising and setting of the sun. In the evening, as darkness fell over the roof of the building in the courtyard I sat on my bed in the south dormitory. Very soon the lamp in Master Kuanji's room went out and he went to sleep with the falling night as the sound of water and of evening birdsong together entered my dreams.

Master Kuanji's hut was a few minutes from that of Mother Honghui and when I reached it she was about to go out but she said that because I had visited so often, she would alter her plans and stay and talk to me.

Mother Honghui had sat at the feet of Master Kuanji as a lay sister for over ten years and had not long taken her vows. The previous year she had been at a large monastery in the south where the masters had wanted to keep her. She said that, rather selfishly, she had hankered after the hills here as well the master whom she had followed for over ten years and had come back.

As to practice and self cultivation she told me that her practice consisted only of reciting the buddhist scriptures. Her hut was now complete and she would soon move in, she thanked all the destinies that had allowed her hut to be completed so smoothly. The day before the hut had finally been finished, two black-billed pica birds had taken up residence in a tree in the courtyard, thus increasing the number of her neighbors.

Honghui took to the kitchen to cook supper and made noodles for us. Her younger brother Kuankui took two of the mountain hill dwellers up to the gulley of the stream above the hut to build a pond. I sat in front of the opening in the stove watching the fire and listening to Mother Honghui as she talked about her hut, while the flames from the burning wood leapt bright and transparent, making me think of the purity of snow.

The telephone installed in the east dormitory rang, it was one of Mother Honghui's colleagues telling her that she was to attend a seven day buddhist service off mountain at the Caotang Temple. She was going to tell practitioners in other huts on the mountain that they could all go down the mountain together the following day. Provided their store of food was sufficient some of those living on the mountain were unwilling to attend these events. Many of the practitioners went off the mountain to put up at a large monastery, when they left there might be a little financial support. I had heard that practitioners on the mountain received financial support every month from a hermit in Hong Kong. Honghui said that only a very small number were able to enjoy this. There were more than 500 people who had become monks or nuns (not including lay buddhists) living on the mountain of whom over 200 received financial support of 80 yuan a month. On the list were those who had been on the mountain early, she wasn't on the list, all this was a matter of following destiny.

Before we eat supper Mother Honghui had to go half-way up the mountain to tell Mother Jieru who lived there that they should go down the mountain together the following day. It was said that the ascetic monk also lived there and I asked Mother Honghui whether I could accompany her.

We crossed a roughly built stone bridge over a stream and saw a thicket of bamboo not far ahead, hanging from the tip of the bamboos was a notice: "Please do not break off, leave alone so that the leaves can hear the humming of the wind." There was Buxiu Maopeng (the Hut of No Practice) above. The mountain door of the hut, beside the stone bridge, was barred by a tree branch with a brush written notice above: "Visitors refused." An old lay brother of fifty or more with a northeastern accent struck up a conversation with Mother Honghui from the other side of the fence.

On the last occasion, we had had the good fortune to break with custom and enter the courtyard, a destiny allowed us by this old lay brother. We had turned over the "Visitors refused" notice that barred the way to the entrance in the fence and hoping for luck had stood at the fence entrance loudly reciting one of the many names of the Buddha, the old lay brother had come out and opened the gate.

Originally, we had been one of the very few visitors to this hut. Normally, when somebody knocked at the door the lay brother sought the consent of the master before opening it and the master very rarely allowed strangers into the courtyard.

The occupant of Buxiu Maopeng was in his thirties and the lay brother who followed him was half as old again. The lay brother's gaze had a radiance which I had not often seen and so had his speech, everything under his gaze seemed as penetrating and clear as spring water.

The hermit said that he had no title, that the hut was his

41

best footnote. He had left home to become a monk in the Southwest in 1999 and had been here ever since.

Realizing that I had come with many questions to ask, he said that if I had questions I was to ask and he might be able to provide answers. I asked: how do you normally practice?

A: The method is unimportant. All rules should be set aside. The rule is that there are no rules. Instruction is merely a path, in the way that the nourishment required for each stage of life is different. Babies eat liquid food and when they have grown eat all kinds of food based on the differing requirements of each stage. The rule is void.

Q: What is void?

A: Zen does not cease to seek answers, the void is not finality, it is all a process. Living in the present is a void.

Q: How can one measure the results of practice in somebody who has become a monk or nun?

A: In this age, seeing whether or not there is achievement is to see whether or not there are ashes in a stupa after death, that is testimony to the practice of morality meditation and wisdom.

Q: Do you plan on spending all your life here?

A: That depends, perhaps I will have gained something and will leave very soon, perhaps I shall stay here all my life and will continue to practice here in the next life.

Q: Why is it that in this day and age some practitioners refuse to give instruction?

A: Perhaps because their own personal cultivation is not complete, or because the time is not yet ripe for you, they have their own reasons. Buddha does not approach those without affinity. Perhaps the diamond seed of those who have no affinity with buddha has not sprouted or has not been planted, if you preach Buddhism to them, they will not believe or will be troubled or even antagonistic.

The occupant of the hut told us that some years ago on a rainy day, the then occupant was sitting in Zen contemplation during a thunderstorm. There was a terrifying clap of thunder, the door was smashed open and a black bear suddenly burst in with its head clasped in its paws and dived trembling into the corner. It didn't leave until the thunder had stopped. Most of all, thunder frightens bears, a thunderclap can frighten them half to death. The hut had become the bear's refuge.

There was a monk strangely clad in a padded jacket and a straw hat sitting in the sun. He took little part in our conversation and just sat there sunbathing. He was the occupant of the hut above who had come down to take tea with the occupant of Buxiu Maopeng. Looking at the Solomon's seal (*polygonatum*) drying on the fence in the sun, I enquired whether it was possible, as in the legends, to eat a little and go for seven days without eating. The monk in the padded jacket joined in to say it was good to eat grain well, one shouldn't be like him. He had got into this state because he had eaten something that he shouldn't when off mountain the previous year. This year he had to survive the summer in a padded jacket.

This time, there was nobody else in the courtyard, just an old lay sister. She said that she didn't want to go down the mountain with Mother Honghui and we continued our climb to the top.

The mountain path was narrow and kept to the stream, it was almost impossible to see whether people had used it, it seemed forgotten and was quickly hidden by weeds and the approach of darkness. The further we went the narrower it became until we finally entered a narrow gully like a stone gate, the path and the stream were squeezed together so that we had to leap from stone to stone on the riverbed as we made our way forward.

A hut without a wall round it appeared, at its foot the water

▲ The ascetic buddhist monk on the rear slope of Nanwutai (Photo / Guo Feng)

from the stream flowed down the mountain. The sound of one of the names of the Buddha emerged from the undergrowth followed by the appearance of a lay sister who was washing clothes on the bank of the stream.

In the courtyard, a practitioner clad in the yellow robe of a monk was working with great concentration, it was the ascetic monk of legend. He had taken his vows at the Caotang temple 20 years ago, this was his home now. His disciple, the nun Jieru, welcomed us and I made a deep obeisance to this ascetic. He did not stop working and just raised his head and greeted us with one of the names of the Buddha. I squatted down in front of this legendary ascetic monk to watch him at work.

He was splitting wood with an axe to make a new handle for a spade. There were various bits and pieces under the awning beside the hut and a wheelbarrow of a sort that nowadays has almost vanished was parked inside. I looked at this ancient hut and voiced my inner misgivings, doesn't this hut leak? It does, he said, but it's no great problem.

His disciple told us that they had recently been busy on repairs, heavy rain had washed away a corner of the bank round the courtyard and they had built it up with rocks. I saw that it had already been filled and leveled with earth.

I asked him how he practiced asceticism here. He said that he didn't, he just lived here and sometimes recited the *Heart Sutra*. Apart from the work in hand he seemed to have no interest in anything else.

Twilight covered the ravine and we were going back down the mountain to Qingjing Maopeng where we would have the evening meal. I looked back from a distance and saw the ascetic monk still working away, it seemed he would not stop, perhaps, in his eyes, there was no such thing as night.

The workers who had been out to build the pond came back in the evening. I sat with the others around the stone table at Qingjing Maopeng and eat a simple meal and then sat on my bed. Mountain dwellers have the same daily schedule as animals, the dogs went to their dens to sleep, the birds were still singing and I was soon dreaming. In the middle of the night the dogs started barking, that should be the bears coming down to drink at the stream below Qingjing Maopeng.

I woke in the morning amidst a chorus of birdsong. A woodpecker was tapping at a tree, sounding like a monk knocking on a wooden fish, though I didn't know whether the woodpecker was reciting a sutra as well. A cuckoo was calling, a clear distant sound with a golden quality.

Jieru was already knocking at the wooden door to the hut when I was still half asleep and deep in the chorus of birdsong. Breakfast was steamed buns, pickled vegetables and noodles.

The food at the hut seemed very filling, after a bowlful I didn't feel hungry for some time.

After breakfast I went down the mountain with Kuanji, Honghui and Jieru. Master Kuanji pointed out the herbs beside the path to me as we descended, there was honeysuckle, poor man's ginseng (codonopsis pilosula) and Solomon's seal, so many that I could not remember their names.

Passing Mother Honghui's new hut she told me that in due course she wanted to build a store house, and buy the walnut trees in the vicinity from the hill dwellers and make the place a real Bodhimanda. When the time came it could be a great convenience to everybody in the area.

At the entrance to the village we waited for the earliest bus down the mountain. In it there were hermits who had come from even deeper in the hills. We were crowded into the swaying bus alongside the chickens and piglets that the hill dwellers were bringing down the mountain. Together we swayed downhill to the clamor of the plain.

At the bus station we changed buses for the Caotang Temple in Hu county, less than a hundred *li* (50 km) from here. The bus drove along a main road with wheat growing on either side and then dropped anchor by a river. The driver grumbled ceaselessly, complaining that the bus wasn't an obedient donkey. We stood at the roadside waiting to continue our journey by the bus on the next shift.

Caotang Temple is an important temple at the foot of the Southern Hills and a major monastery in the history of Buddhism. With Master Kuanji I visited the site of the famous "Caotang mist", a well head amongst bamboos that emitted mist all the year round. Legend has it that a dragon used to live in the well and that the mist from its mouth ascended the well and joined the clouds in the nearby Southern Hills, making it one of the eight sights of the Guanzhong plain. But that was a long time ago and the dragon may have flown away. The mist no longer spurts from the well head and an octagonal monument has been erected, its face carved with some ancient literary figure's praise and fascination for the "Caotang mist".

I had planned to leave and return to the bustling city after visiting all the statues of buddha. Honghui and the others had all registered to stay in the guest quarters of the monastery and attend a seven day buddhist service.

Kuanji insisted on seeing me off and came with me as far as the junction with the main road outside the temple where we saluted each other and parted. As I turned away towards the road, to my surprise, feelings of loss welled up, like sudden banks of cloud in a clear sky.

A wind sprang up and blew the dust from the road upwards. I turned and looked at the back of Kuanji as he gradually retreated into the distance and then a cloud of dust obscured my vision.

Countless hermits are concentrated on the rear slopes of Nanwutai and in the steep neighboring valleys. Many have come from a distance and have chosen to begin their lives as hermits there. According to Mother Honghui there is an ascetic hermit who has lived for more than ten years on the banks of the river in the gorge at Shibianyu. He goes barefoot without trace no matter what the season and very few local people have ever seen him. I imagined meeting that legendary practitioner on a narrow path deep in the forest.

At Chang'an bus station I took the direct bus service to Qingcha. Seeing the buddhist beads on the wrist of the driver I struck up a conversation with him. The driver was a lay buddhist who had met the legendary bare-foot monk hermit, he said that it was easier to get into heaven than to find him. He suggested that I should take no risks, it was impossible to find the place where he lived, there were basically no roads.

He was unwilling to reveal the location. He had been driving in and out of the hills for over ten years, I guessed that he held many more mountain secrets that he was unwilling to divulge. Ever since people had learned of the existence of the bare-foot monk a few years earlier, many had gone to look for him and the hills were no longer tranquil.

The bus stopped in front of a cluster of clay built houses beside the road. There was no sign for the terminus stop, no vehicle could reach the track into the depths of the steep mountain valleys. It was only possible on foot and I intended to reach the huts that lay deepest in the valleys and to start my visiting from there.

The valley path followed the river upwards. At a distance of 70 *li* from the edge of the hills the river was much larger than the one I had seen at the entrance to the valley. The sound of the water shook the heavens and as I walked beside the river I could hear nothing beyond the sound of the water. The river had taken on the color of the hills, a gleaming green, the stones at the bottom clearly visible.

The first village up from Qingcha was Xianrencha, the place where the legendary bare-foot monk had appeared. Further up was Laolongqiao with all the hill dwellers houses built beside the river and the river water flowing past in the shadow of the houses. There is a stone bridge over the river.

I asked the way of a young hill dweller beside the river, he said that the local village chief was a hermit who knew all about the huts hereabouts. There were a large number of huts deep in a valley west of the stone bridge, many practitioners who came here from outside usually visited the village chief first.

At noon I dragged my shadow alone along the mountain path with cobblestones underfoot that were the size of a fist and pressed achingly into my feet as I walked.

Laolongqiao was the last village in the valley. I sat in a

roadside shop eating instant noodles and the proprietress told me that the old people in the village said that there was a natural cave in the valley opposite where a hermit called Master Dayu had lived before 1949. Before becoming a monk he had been Vice Minister of Education under the Beiyang government and Nan Huaijin had been his pupil for a while in Sichuan during the war against Japan. No one knew how many years he had lived there. Later when people from outside came to visit the hermit, he had already disappeared without trace.

I looked up at the hill opposite and could see only a vague silhouette of the gorge and could hardly see its entrance, cloud and mist obscured the higher peaks in a vast haze.

After finishing the noodles I continued on my way, the proprietress told me that not far after passing the last house there was a gorge that ran eastwards, this was Dabancha, beyond that point there was no road.

I followed the directions. The mountain became steeper and steeper and the valley deeper, the sound of the water swirled between the two banks and then flew skywards. This was a metalled road especially cut through for transport vehicles with some of it cut into the hillside. With the vast mountain overhead, the woods of pine and cypress seemed even more mysterious in the dusk. Apart from the sun on the mountain crests the rest seemed as black as night. There was nobody at all on the road, just birds flying past, I longed to see a pedestrian drifting by, even a hill dweller to ask the way would do.

It was six o'clock in the afternoon, there still seemed no end to this road and I suspected that I had already passed the gorge leading to Dabancha. I began to worry about not being able to find somewhere to spend the night. The green of the forest was turning deep black and the setting sun was turning the distant peaks to gold when a lorry carrying stone drove by, I shouted at it frantically but the sound was completely drowned by the motor.

The lorry drove on past leaving me covered in smoky dust and despair.

I thought that if I couldn't find Dabancha I would turn back and after dark reach the village where I had eaten noodles and try and find a bed for the night. There was nobody ahead as I walked on and I didn't know where to go.

After drinking the last mouthful of water in my flask I started to jog back down the road and once out of the deep gorge I could see the sun, its slanting rays shining on the mountain slope as coldly as the moon.

Finally as I rounded the top of a hill I saw a young woman standing beside a vehicle at the side of the road and I asked her the way. She was lay sister Miao and said that her teacher would come by and could answer my questions.

It was a secret gorge where two streams joined, the river waters flowed out from the gorge and because the bed of the stream was flat there was very little sound. The track into the gorge was completely submerged in the stream. The river bank was thickly covered with trees and without a guide, standing on the bank it would be impossible to see the gorge beside you.

A motorbike came driving down from the other side of the stream in the gorge, the middle aged rider had a long beard and a smile as comfortable as a breeze in spring. What piqued my curiosity was the fact that he was wearing sandals. Sister Miao said this was Master Changshu. I rejoiced that I had a bed for the night, the mercy of the Buddha would not leave me out in the wild.

There was no bridge and no stones in the river upon which it was possible to leap across. The river was deep and it was already November and cold. Master Changshu had just returned from buying building material off mountain. Sister Miao and I mounted the pillion of the motorbike. The road was on the bed of the river and the bike crossed through the water which came up to our knees. I realized why Master Changshu wore sandals.

The hut was not far from the river and was still under construction. There was a small structure by the river that housed the generator for the hut. There was a constant strong current in the river throughout the seasons and no lack of electricity for the hut.

The hut was under a cliff half-way up the mountain and over the entrance was an inscription "Puxian Lanruo"—temple of the Puxian Buddha. There was a small peaceful temple containing three buddhas by the entrance with green silk hanging at its door. A motorized tricycle loaded with timber was parked at the entrance and the courtyard was filled with people. There were several hill dwellers at work and two rather elderly hermits. We all unloaded the timber and afterwards I followed Hermit Miao to the rear courtyard to drink tea.

The hut was built like a bird's nest, its rear wall was the bed rock of the cliff. The shape of the cliff resembled a crescent moon and faced southwards towards the hills. There was a mountain spring above the roof which flowed to the rear courtyard through a cloister under the cliff which was planted with flourishing bamboo that almost burst through the roof. There were six brick and tile rooms in the front courtyard and another six in the rear. The glass in the windows was as transparent as crystal. All the plants in the courtyard were bamboo.

The tea was the best Iron Buddha and the water was piped down from the spring over the roof, they said that when it rained the roof became a waterfall, the water from the cliff flowing from here through the courtyard and on down to the river.

My room was in the rear courtyard, it had a desk, a toilet and the bed was very comfortable and but for the lack of television it would have been as good as a hotel.

When I graded all the huts in the Southern Hills in my mind I discovered that this was without a doubt the best built, some people said that Lianchi Maopeng was a five-star hut, in that case this was six stars.

I told Changshu of my view and he burst out laughing and said that it would be absolutely unforgivable not to practice well in an environment like this. He and his disciple and followers lived here, I think Sister Miao and the two elderly lay people were their family.

They had lived here many years, had begun building three years ago and had just completed a phase. Master Changshu had become a buddhist ten years previously in Lushan and had later moved here—the place where Master Dayu had lived as a hermit. Going even further back, there had always been practitioners here, it was a good place to practice. Master Changshu told me that in the mountains, there was a subtle and mysterious relationship between man and nature. There was a mutuality between your moral sense and your appreciation of nature. There were people who arrived somewhere and spring water suddenly appeared in waterless environments and there were others whose arrival in a favorable environment banished the benevolent *fengshui*.

He said that at Guanyinshan, the disciples of Master Yuanzhao continued to practice near his place of practice and that black bears often came to the entrance to bring them firewood.

Daoist monks lived deeper in this gorge much further up along the river, Master Changshu urged me not to undertake the journey lightly, it was almost impossible to find and easy to get lost. He had seen people coming out from deep in the next gorge down, but there was no track there. I estimated that from here to the depths of the gorge would take several days on foot and I might not get there.

Daoist practitioners generally chose to live in caves close to the top of mountains that could only be reached by birds or mountain mice, there were no paths passable to man and it was impossible for an ordinary person to find them.

Perhaps because it had been made with spring water the Iron Buddha tea tasted exceptionally sweet and two pots were soon finished. After the evening meal Changshu's disciples and followers went off to meditate. The moon appeared in the clouds above the mountain peak opposite, growing like a seed, a horn of the crescent shining out bit by bit and slowly increasing more and more so that the pine trees on the top of the mountain cast their own shadow on the moon. The noise of the stream below the hut sounded silvery in the moonlight like a hermit's *qin* or the tinkle of chimes.

Changshu said that there was no permanence to life, adhering to buddhist discipline and undertaking practice was as pressing and urgent as if one's hair was on fire. The 24 channels of Chinese medicine are actually the knots of human thought. The more enlightened you become the more the channels open. At present, self cultivation had to do with tugging one's mind back from the external world and refocusing it on the self so as to become acquainted with one's body and the "me" that lives within it. Throughout our lives we mistakenly believe that the body is "me", the body is "my" body but it is not "me". Our whole life long, we eat for it, clothe it, make it comfortable, take it to the doctor, and when we are old we are trapped by it, suffer for it and when we are free of it, we still believe that "it" is oneself. If we lived in the body of an animal we would believe that the animal was "self" and that we would be re-incarnated for life after life and age after age.

The calm of Zen was like the water of a lake, the calmer it was the fewer the impurities and the fewer the impurities the more clearly the bottom of the lake was visible, the degree of calm determined the degree of the profundity of Zen calm.

Master Changshu said that normally the gate to the hut was kept closed and they had little contact with the outside world. Every winter they started Zen retreats which lasted for seven days at a time during which they meditated all night until dawn, sometimes there were seven retreats in succession.

That night I sat on my bed in meditation and then fell asleep to the sound of the water in the gulley. At four o'clock next morning Master Changshu's disciples started practicing *taijiquan* in the courtyard. I then followed by starting to drink the tea that had not been infused the night before.

After a breakfast of dry buns and pickles, I shouldered my pack and clasping my hands bowed in farewell to the three practitioners. Master Changshu's disciples smiled at my salutation. There was a deep meaning to their smile and they returned my greeting without a buddhist salutation. They were not at all concerned with outward form.

As it happened, Master Changshu needed to go down the mountain for business and I had a free trip. Once over the river I had a ride in his Jeep back to the place where I had eaten instant noodles the previous day.

I sat at the same table as before and asked the proprietress for a bowl of noodles, a minute later I had eaten the lot. I asked this villager the way to Meihuadong (Peach Blossom Cave). She gave me detailed directions. I learned from her that the master who had used to live there had left and a monk from the Wolong Temple had just arrived. Some people had gone up a few days ago. I thanked her and set out immediately.

I really needed to find a guide but the villagers thought, perhaps, that the fee was too small and nobody displayed any interest. I would have to rely on myself. This was yet another remote hill gorge with vegetation so luxuriant that I had to part it with my staff before I could get through. A lot of white funerary money had been scattered on the route, there is no permanence in life or death, nowhere is forgotten, even the deep mountains.

At a point where the valley widened slightly a grave mound blocked the way ahead and the path disappeared. Apart from a stream and the dense grass there was no trace of man and the grass was so thick that I could be submerged in it. I looked all around fruitlessly and had to return and sit by the grave. How I hoped that the person lying there had been alive, if so there would have been somebody to ask the way and somebody to talk to. In my mind, I began to recite the *Ksitigarbha Sutra* for the deceased in the hope that he could give me directions.

After reciting the sutra, I tried to find the path again and found it, a faint track on the other side of the stream seemingly made by animals. I did not have too many reservations, in the depths of this uninhabited gorge I could only go forward.

On the unpeopled mountain, the water flowed and the flowers bloomed and there were traces of trampled grass. As I followed the river valley the path sometimes appeared on the stones under the water; in the upper reaches of the stream it couldn't be seen at all, the all embracing undergrowth had gone and all that remained were the trees and rocks that covered the whole valley.

The gorge became narrower and narrower and at some places was only a few meters across. The sky could only be seen with difficulty and all that could be seen overhead was the black green shadow of the mountains.

Eventually, I saw a row of stones arranged across a water meadow, they had obviously been transported there and in the rainy season they formed a bridge, the stones were the only sign of mankind that could be found in this remote valley. I crossed the blocks of stone and sat down for a rest. I was encouraged to see a file of figures emerging from the distant depths of the valley. Coming towards me were two lay buddhists and a monk. I asked them the way and the monk's answer made me sigh with dejection. He said there was no point in going on, there was nobody up at the caves, the Meihuadong was locked and there was nobody at the Heifengdong, the occupants had all gone down the mountain. They themselves had just come for a walk.

There was nothing for it but to go back down the mountain with them. The mountain here was called Wufengshan (Five Peaks) and was said to have two natural caves, Meihuadong above and Heifengdong below, they were two of the oldest caves in the Southern Hills, where countless practitioners had lived in the past, some had lived there all their lives. There had been no banknotes, no complicated personal relationships and no appetizing food, just birds and beasts, white cloud and cool wind. It seemed the sort of almost trackless mountain that nobody would be willing to spend time climbing or that would fail to interest even outdoor hobby- climbing back-packers.

On the way I struck up a conversation with the monk. He was unwilling to divulge his title. I expressed my regret at not having met the occupant of the Meihuadong. He then said that actually he was the occupant and I was embarrassed at my own clumsiness.

Because there were more people the path did not seem as long as it had done going up and we were out of the gorge in about two hours. My eyes had difficulty adapting to the brilliant sunshine in the valley. Bidding farewell to the master of the Meihuadong I returned to the little shop and had another bowl of instant noodles. The proprietress was no longer a stranger. I asked her again about huts in the neighborhood. She said that there was a track which led eastwards from the north of the village further down. That was Xianrencha where the bare-foot monk of legend lived. However, she said that she had not seen him for about six months and seemed not to have seen him come off the mountain.

Despite not having found a guide I decided to try my luck again.

I dragged myself on under the noonday sun. The hill dwellers were having a midday nap and not even a dog was to be seen in the village. I was almost bent double by the heat of the sun but felt a little better after a drink of water. My feet and legs felt disconnected from the rest of my body, leaving only mechanical movement.

In this valley, the grass was not high and only came up to waist height. I looked at my shadow on the mountain path and imagined that the bare-foot monk had passed along here, his clothing would have been ragged and he was bound to be very thin.

I moved on, tapping the rocks beside the path with my staff as I went, at noon there were more than the normal number of snakes about and I should tell them I was in the hills. The grass in the valley wasn't growing terribly well and between the trees and the grass there were white rocks, bigger than the room of a house, I constantly thought that one of them was the dwelling place of the bare-foot monk but seeing the path stretching forward without a turning, I carried on. Where the valley began to divide, the grass grew profusely, there were ancient vines thicker than my arm and huge fallen trees rotting in the grass which almost engulfed me. My staff wasn't much use, the grass was so high that it was difficult to part it. In the undergrowth there was a very small abandoned hut.

At the place where the path through the grass started to diverge I entered a different gorge.

As I climbed up through the gorge towards the top of the mountain, I saw no sign at all that anybody had passed through. The sun was almost invisible and the narrow gorge was completely covered by a canopy of trees. The ground was covered with pine cones and pine needles and spring water flowed beside the path.

At the foot of a huge rock I saw a memorial shrine to a deceased hermit built with small stones on the top of a rock. It stood calmly amongst the soughing pines, I could see no inscription and it was of unknown date.

Further up, the terrain leveled out and a stone building appeared. I was pleasurably surprised but instantly deflated as I approached. The door was not locked and I pushed open the wooden door to see that it was a cave with a stone entrance and windows built out from the cave mouth. The cave contained a heatable brick bed as well as painted figures of the Buddha and broken pottery. The holy names of the Buddha were written on the walls. There were traces of water in a corner, it was too damp and green moss was growing. There were deer droppings all over the floor. Some years ago, or perhaps some hundreds of years ago, this cave had been a hermit's paradise.

With the name "Xianrencha" on my lips I began to follow another path to the hills. As a result, I soon discovered that the path underfoot had not been made by man, it was formed from the hoof prints of animals and I tripped on the grass into an enormous pile of dried animal dung. Perhaps the trees that covered the mountain were laughing at my mishap.

I began to retrace my steps back down the mountain. I was building bricks without straw, I had not met the bare-foot monk and hadn't even seen a corner of his clothing, all I had to show were the words "bare-foot monk".

The sun had disappeared behind the mountain, the valley had turned pitch-black and I was about to be defeated by exhaustion. In the end, I returned to Laolongqiao, a hamlet beside a stream where I was going to try and find a bed for the night.

At the entrance to the village, from a distance, I saw four buddhists wearing conical bamboo hats and carrying buckets. I greeted them, there was a tunnel being bored deep in the valley and they were going up to the site to work in exchange for living expenses.

I asked them where they practiced and they pointed to the village beside the stream and we both continued on our opposite ways. I had heard that there were a number of huts in the gorge to the west of Laolongqiao and I thought I would spend the night there.

There were several old people sitting on the steps in the village and I asked one of them, a peasant woman, the way up the mountain. She took me through her courtyard and told me that many people in the village were hermits. Following her directions, I started to climb the mountain intending to climb as far as Tianchi Temple, where there were supposed to be several rooms. Night fell and on all sides the mountains seemed indistinct. Rounding a bend on the shoulder of the mountain I found two monks sitting in meditation on the top of a large rock with their staves laid beside them. I stopped to ask them the way and they said that there were very many huts in the gorge but I would find it very difficult to find anywhere to stay the night, nobody was willing to offer accommodation to a stranger. By this time, it was impossible to reach the Tianchi Temple and, moreover, I had no means of lighting my way.

My heart fell and I seemed to see myself standing at the perimeter of the huts in the gorge but with nowhere to rest my head, their warning made me realize that I was an unfamiliar intruder on this mountain.

I said goodbye to them and started back down the mountain and eventually reached the entrance to the village in the darkness. I thought that I would only obtain accommodation by finding the village chief. Following the direction pointed out to me by one of the villagers I came across one of the village chief's family, the chief was away, I explained my purpose but the attitude displayed towards me made me realize that I really was unwelcome here.

It was already dark and there was no vehicle going off mountain. I began to be anxious about overnight accommodation.

At the entrance to the village I enquired of one of the old people still sitting on the steps whether there was anywhere in the village where I could spend the night. She said that there were no surplus rooms for people to stay and, besides, I was a stranger.

I then returned to the village chief's house which I had just passed, where a number of people were gathered. I asked a young man where I could hire a vehicle to take me down the mountain—I'd seen him come out of the village chief's house and guessed that he would be familiar with the locality. He agreed to arrange a vehicle for me.

He started to telephone a vehicle owner in a village upstream, the fare would be 100 yuan to take me back down the mountain to Xi'an. It would be over an hour before the vehicle arrived.

I asked an old person at the entrance to the village whether I could borrow a bench to sit and wait for the vehicle.

The old lady sighed when she learned that the fare down the mountain was 100 yuan, had she known I could have stayed in her house for nothing, but now a fellow villager had helped and arranged a vehicle for me. She was on the point of tears and said that she was 89 this year and had been a buddhist for a score of years and more, now this had happened. She unceasingly clasped her hands in remorse. The vehicle soon arrived and the young man who had helped arrange it hitched a ride with me down the mountain. Before I got on the old

▶ Buddhist monks at Lianchi Maopeng (the Lotus Pool Straw Hut) on the rear slope of Nanwutai (Photo/Guo Feng)

lady implored me, when next I was in the mountains, to stay with her, her family had a further three houses upstream and if buddhist masters wanted to stay they could do so for free for a long time.

The old lady stood there as the vehicle drove into the distance.

One day, Mother Honghui telephoned to say that the opening ceremony for her hut had already been held, it was to be called Hongji Chanshe (Hongji Zen House) and she hoped that this ordinary hut would promote the teachings of Sakamunyi and could shelter more people who wanted to be practitioners. Although it was small it could provide limited help for itinerant practitioners. She hoped that I would go and stay for a few days.

Once more I found myself sitting at the dinner table at Hongji Chanshe. After lunch and hearing lay brother Kuankui say that the occupant of Lianchi Maopeng was at home, I set out on a visit without a moment's hesitation. I began climbing in the direction of Lianchi Maopeng on its mountain ridge. The path lay deep in the gorge past the houses of two hill dwellers. The last time I had been here, I had come across a peasant woman who told me that on the way to Lianchi Maopeng there was another monk's hut. Because of his skill in Chinese medicine he was often called off mountain to visit the sick.

The path was covered in pine cones and very many were stock-piled by squirrels. The sandy soil of the path was slippery and I selected a tree branch as a staff. After crossing two ridges I finally saw Lianchi Maopeng's red roof and whitewashed walls on the peak of the mountain.

Lianchi Maopeng was built on a ridge facing in the direction of the rising sun. I knocked on the closed door, there was no response. I recited the names of the Buddha there was no movement and I began to shout the title of Master Kuanfa. This time the door opened and a young monk appeared, he said that Master Kuanfa was not there, there were only working people there. However, I insisted and he probably thought that if he didn't let me in I would stay at the entrance, unwilling to leave. He then let me in saying, "Tell me if there's anything you want, I'm a simple man and not at all complicated."

The hut's courtyard was very large and at the cliff edge there was no surrounding wall on any side. Huts could be dimly seen on the opposite ridge. There were several workers in the courtyard. Master Kuanfa had said that he was going to remodel the drinking water facilities so as to provide drinking water for several hundred people. Following that, he was going to establish a Zen study center. The ground here was quite wide, a plateau that he had built up, stone by stone, since he arrived, it had previously been a hollow in the mountain. He was mulling over the idea of the biggest Zen center in the mountains and was going to pay to recruit students to come and practice. Buddhist teaching was very active in the area, as long as people came to study and practice Buddhism the center would be responsible for everything until they graduated.

Amongst his practitioner colleagues was Kailong, former abbot of the Jingye Temple and a graduate of Peking University, another was the current abbot, Master Benru.

He said that as long you wanted to do something, money wasn't a problem. His family had been the soap king of Shanghai and at the age of six he had told his mother that he wanted to build a house in the Southern Hills and live there. The family had been frightened that he would leave home to become a buddhist but when he had reached the age of maturity and could make his own decisions he had finally donned a monk's robe.

He had arrived here with only just over 30 yuan and had bought a sack of potatoes which he had carried up the mountain on his back. He had lived on potatoes every day.

Brother Kuankui said that he had meditated through the nights here for three years.

In a state of meditative calm he had seen himself as he had been several hundred years previously. He said that in his former life he had still been a buddhist monk but then he had expounded the teachings of the buddhist law and now he recited the names of the Buddha, one name would last all night.

As I was leaving, Master Kuanfa asked me how long I recited the names of the Buddha for, he said that unless I could recite for 12 hours a day, there was very little that we could talk about. Finally he taught me how to recite and a stream of the names of the Buddha flowed from his throat like spring water, before one stream of names had ended another stream sounded on the outward breath so that he was reciting both as he inhaled and as he exhaled. That was a single cycle of recitation. He said that this was the way that Master Yinguang had used to recite. It was like a necklace of pearls of the Buddha, one should string them together, they should not be broken.

At the entrance Master Kuanfa pointed to the range of hills to the east and said that Master Zangyuan had lived here the longest and was well skilled in practice. I should go and call on him, he was the "*Lao Da*"—the chief one of all here.

Buoyed up by the title "*Lao Da*" I went down the mountain to call on the Qingliang Maopeng .

Down the mountain ridge and over the river and following the directions of Master Kuanfa I climbed up from the depths of the gorge, it was getting dark as I passed the Buxiu Maopeng and the old lay sister that I had seen last time was in the courtyard. Despite the fact that it was already dusk, she recognized me at once. When she knew that I was going on up to Qingliang Maopeng, she said that I had arrived just at the right moment, there was an off mountain letter for Master Zangyuan and I could take it up.

The letter was most opportune and could help me knock at the entrance to Master Zangyuan's hut even though I might not get in. Master Kuanfa had said that Master Zangyuan was an old practitioner who very rarely went off mountain and did not have much to do with his fellow practitioners. He spoke little and was reluctant to meet people. Whether or not this letter would induce Master Zangyuan to start talking and expound the way would depend upon whether I was lucky today.

The gorge took a turn round the bottom of a cliff and a deeper gorge appeared hidden in the depths of a forest. In a depression I saw the ascetic monk's hut, this time the door was locked. I had seen him again in the main hall of the Xingjiao Temple before I came up the mountain. Because of his long residence in the mountains his legs had been afflicted with severe rheumatism and he was now looking after the hall there, I guessed it would be a long time before he could live in the hills again.

It was already dark, and in the gorge the path suddenly disappeared. The grass was very high and once I stepped into it was very difficult to take the other step out. I had to retreat and search carefully in the gorge. Eventually I found a small hut above the ascetic monk's hut and I scrambled out of the grass up to the hut's courtyard. Sitting on a bench in front of two low doors to the hut was Mother Jieru, chanting the sutras. My sudden appearance startled her, she said that she was in seclusion here. Surprisingly, despite the darkness she could make out the sutra text, I was astonished.

The path had been cut off by her courtyard and she had blocked the path on either side with a fence. She said Master Yanxin's hut was waiting for a master coming in to the hills to stay. She opened the fence and let me out and closed it behind me. If I hadn't been able to use this hut as a reference point I would have been in a mess.

Feeling my way along the path in the darkness I was worried that wild boar might block the way. If they demanded that I should leave a leg or other part of my body as a toll fee I would be in no position to refuse, I felt my heart beating like a drum as if it were urging me on. The evening breeze was cool and the moon was already up when I reached the top.

Qingliang Maopeng stood between some ruins and a vegetable patch but I couldn't find the gate. As I approached, I recited the names of the Buddha in front of a window as a greeting to Master Zangyuan in the darkness within. After circling the building, I at last found the entrance on top of the cliff, it was closed but as the bearer of a letter I went in.

What made me curious was that Master Zangyuan's face seemed to glow in the dark, his complexion was so good that it made those from off the mountain envious. He sat in the darkness and started reading the letter as soon as I entered the room.

He had lived here for over ten years, he said that living in the hills was actually very simple. He really didn't like talking.

There is a dispute amongst lay buddhists, many people, in their first contact with Buddhism, have difficulty understanding the scriptures and quickly lose patience and interest, they need to rely on an upright and moral guide who can teach them the correct way. But nowadays, where can such people be found? Consequently, many are bewildered and do not know how to set about properly structured practice. This was the problem I wished to put to Master Zangyuan.

Master Zangyuan pointed out that one should first obtain enlightenment through reciting the names of the Buddha and then read the scriptures. One should recite until you reached a state of tranquil emptiness which was void of notion and concentrate the individual consciousness upon experiencing the personal internal and external stimuli of the immediate instant in time, and then use this state to replace thought and

▲ A practitioner descending the rear slopes of Nanwutai to buy supplies
(Photo / Wang Xinyong)

the drawing of distinctions between things. Once skilled to the point of naturally acquired wisdom any scripture can be read with unobstructed understanding at first sight.

Master Zangyuan's voice was clear and resonant and when it dropped darkness returned to the eyes once more. There had been many problems that I had wished to put to him but at this stage I was devoid of thought.

I thought that if I could spend the night here with Master Zangyuan, I might perhaps continue to seek instruction. When I suggested this to Master Zangyuan he said that he could find me a place in another room but that he was going to meditate through the night, he had already said enough today.

I saw that this was as far as I could take it. I then bid him farewell and prepared to go down the mountain and spend the night at the Hongji Chanshe.

As I was leaving, Master Zangyuan asked me to take some apples down the mountain with me to give to Mother Honghui and the abstinent master at the Buxiu Maopeng, as well as a bunch of green vegetables that he had grown, he would never be able to finish eating his vegetables. I then set off down the mountain with a bunch of vegetables and a sack of apples on my back.

As luck would have it, on the way up Mother Honghui had pressed a torch on me otherwise I might have rolled down the mountain. At the bottom of the gorge I called to Mother Jieru to open the fence that barred the way, gave her some apples and continued on my way down. I reached the Hongji Chanshe, eat the evening meal that had long been waiting for me and went to sleep.

The following morning after eating noodles I determined to find the hut that I had passed two years previously. It was in a gorge not far further down. Below the hut there was a millstone, two monks lived there.

I eventual found the hut of my memory below a large millstone beside the path, it hadn't changed at all. There was a terrace in front of the entrance and various kinds of vegetable were planted beside the building. There were apple and peach trees below the terrace.

The door was closed and the windows were roughly boarded up with nailed slats. Looking in through the window I could see it was dark inside. I recited the names of the Buddha from outside the window and a very faint sound came from inside which I thought was a carpenter bee in the window. In a moment, the sound moved from this window to another I thought that it ought to be the sound of a monk chanting the sutras. I stood still in front of the door and after a long while it opened to reveal the monk whom I had met several months earlier wearing a cotton robe, now clad in a monk's robe suitable to the season.

He recognized me. He said that he had lived here for years and had never had anything to do with people from off the mountain, normally when visitors arrived he escaped to another hut on the ridge. Several months previously there had been a hermit who had found him and spent a great deal of money in a large hospital off mountain to have his sickness cured. He now lived in this hill dwellers house, there were a large number of these empty uninhabited houses, and you could live in any one of them, he was helping the hill dwellers by looking after this one. Everybody else built new huts but that spent the hermits money and all hermits were poor, he was of no fixed abode but that did not affect his practice.

He was unwilling to divulge his buddhist name, but I knew one of his other names, with other buddhists he was known as the "Lazy Monk". So I asked him do you know who the "Lazy Monk" is?

He smiled candidly and said that they took pleasure from calling him that, there were very few who knew his buddhist name. During the many years before he had come here he had visited many places in Tibet and met many people of great achievement. Here he was without fixed abode and his whereabouts uncertain, nobody knew what he was doing, he needed to maintain his distance from people.

The sun shone on the opposite cliff and it was time to prepare the morning vegetarian meal. He turned away to the vegetable patch and took an extra cabbage, his staple diet. The grass grew tall in the empty space in front of the hut, I recognized pigweed which the hill dwellers called *huihuicai* and which can often be seen beside the road and on the ridges between fields. These wild herbs were a major component of the lazy monk's cookery book, and these few waist-high *huihuicai* were picked often but grew well.

Just as we were picking the pigweed, a bunch of backpackers came up behind us intending to take a rest on the terrace. Several of the younger ones passed beside me, stood on the rock and without a care in the world set about picking Lazy Monk's apples. These apples ripened in the autumn and were still sour and green. They seemed to regard Lazy Monk, who was standing in front of me, as transparent. Just as I was about to go and stop them, Lazy Monk indicated that I should take no notice. He said that if I tried to stop them, it would make them angry with me, because they would think that I was preventing them from eating, I could see that the apples weren't ripe.

Once a tourist had even angrily questioned him, saying that it was strange, why had all you people come up to the mountains. Were you frightened of somebody finding you? Lazy Monk said that when he met these sort of people he went up to the mountain ridge, he couldn't allow himself to be angry and upset on their account.

Following him round the hillside I saw the hut where that mountain monk had been living six months earlier. He had gone to a place even deeper in the mountains that nobody could find. Despite the fact it was already sufficiently secluded here, he had felt that it was not enough and his hut was now a place that Lazy Monk looked after.

It seemed really peaceful here, the bamboo beneath the hut flourished, a cool breeze blew on all sides and spring water flowed alongside the bamboo grove.

Lazy Monk took me on a tour, the hut was extremely tidy without a speck of dust. Everything had the color and luster of stone. Over the entrance were a number of notices: "Please do not disturb," "Sacred site for meditation," "No entry to tourists" and many others.

Chapter Three

The Ziwu Valley
—The Kindling of Daoism and a Thatched Hut

In June I shouldered my knapsack once again and passed through the village of Beidoujiao on my way to the Ziwu valley. By the town of Ziwu, at the foot of the mountain, I came across a stream whose source lay far up the valley.

In terms of the Southern Hills, Ziwu valley is at its center, it doesn't have the luxuriance of the narrow valley of the Feng River, it has no concrete or asphalt roads but in ancient times it was on the main route from Sichuan province to the Guanzhong plain. Roadhouses and inns with red lanterns now lie along the unmade road that runs through the villages up into the valley, black-trunked persimmon trees with tender green leaves grow in profusion behind wooden fences, horses graze in leisure beneath the trees and as you look up you can see the pale blue of the Southern Hills. Were it not for the trouble I would even have ridden into the hills on a horse.

The mountain road snaked upwards along the course of the river. As I passed a dried out reservoir I caught up with a hill dweller making his way upwards. His home was in Qiliping in the depths of the valley where there were several homesteads. He had just returned from buying supplies off mountain. There was nobody else to be seen amidst the scent of flowers and the sound of water on this mountain road and so we became traveling companions.

The hill dweller told me that if you turned east along this valley you came to the valley of Baolongyu and the Zhixiang Temple, the founding temple of the Avatamsaka School of Chinese Buddhism. As the road and the river turned a bend, hill dwellers' houses appeared on either side. Built of mud brick they were surrounded by persimmon trees and there appeared to be some abandoned houses by the side of the road.

Beside the river, there seemed to be about ten or more houses, all occupied by elderly people. The young lived down on the plain but the old were reluctant to give up living on the mountain and here they patiently awaited the end of their lives. Along another perspiring stretch of road and the river turned to a waterfall. There was a stone-built temple at the side of the road in which the statue of the Dragon King had lived but all that could be seen now was its base.

Over a stone bridge into another valley where a strangely shaped peak suddenly projected upwards, the hill dwellers called it Shuzhuangtai, the dressing table. In ancient times somebody had once seen a fox fairy sitting on it, grooming itself. When dawn approached and the cock crowed it disappeared. Below this peak was the famous daoist temple Jinxianguan.

During the Tang dynasty, in the middle of the 9th century, the Korean scholar Kim Gagi from the kingdom of Silla, arrived loaded with books to study in Chang'an. Having received a "tributary guest's doctorate" he did not embark on an official career but instead became a hermit in the Ziwu valley where he met Zhongli Quan, one of the eight Daoist Immortals, who taught him the techniques of daoist alchemy. Many years later, Kim returned to Silla and spread the seeds of Daoism where they took root and flourished. In 858, Kim Gagi ascended to immortality at the daoist temple Jinxianguan where the founding temple of Korean Daoism now is.

I parted from the hill dweller at the crossroads by the Jinxianguan Daoist Temple and carried on my way. The path was only about a foot wide and there was a mountain spring below it. At noon, millions of blue and white butterflies formed a cloud and settled on the road and beside the spring where, if you did not look carefully, you might think that with their wings folded upright they were flowers or mushrooms growing there. I had to stamp my foot to warn them to give way before I could pass.

The stream and the path patiently turned and twisted onwards in the center of the gorge so that walking the path was like following a vine towards a melon. A black obstruction appeared across the path in front, it seemed to move. I trembled and my first reaction was: snake! An awareness that made my hair stand on end. Although I was born in the year of the snake, it was still snakes that most frightened me. I was about five paces from it. The snake was by no means small and completely occupied a track that was wide enough to take a vehicle. Its body was as thick as my arm and it lay there motionless. I stopped by the side of the track and recited the titles of the Ksitigarbha Bodhisattva to myself. I believed that the Bodhisattva was bound to help me because I always recite his name when I had the time.

Suddenly, the snake turned completely round and the man-high grass at the side of the track emitted a hissing sound, the grass was still hissing even when the snake had gone some distance. In a while, the waving grass tops moved further and further away and at last it had gone. My blood resumed its circulation and I carried on, praying to the Bodhisattva to save me from another meeting with the snake.

Further on, past the place where I had met the snake I saw several hill dwellers' houses built of mud-brick. Two old people were sitting in the doorway of a two roomed house that had a battered sign hanging from its wall on which was written: Qiliping Primary School. The school had long ago moved down to the plain.

I bought a staff from an old lady, the grass either side of the track grew too thickly but with the staff I didn't need to worry about treading on a snake. I had also heard from another old person that six years earlier a daoist master had been living as a hermit in the depths of the gorge. Accompanied by the staff I continued on my way.

There were several hill dwellers' houses ahead. The path crossed a courtyard where a dog lay on the ground looking at me but not seeing me. The stretch of path that followed was basically squeezed between large rocks and moved further and further away from the river. In some places there was a precipitous cliff at the edge of the path which became narrower and narrower, so that my feet seemed rather too large as they trod it. The track was often obscured by grass and I could only move forward by pushing it aside with my staff. In a while, the track returned to the river valley and I finally saw the stone bridge that the hill dweller had mentioned but it was very small and I leaped directly across the stream to the opposite bank. The path began to divide and a small path that lead eastwards drew me towards a tiny gully that seemed almost beyond discovery.

The gully was much too narrow and but for its stream could easily have been overlooked, it was also concealed by bushes and trees. The path was hidden amidst the grass and dense trees and, as ever, fluctuated above and below the river. Where the path was high up the sound of the water echoed loudly in the deep valley and kapok blossomed with a faint scent amongst the undergrowth at the side of the path.

Butterflies suddenly converged and dispersed and above the sides of the valley white clouds flowed across the sky like water, each layer clearly visible. Alone on this hidden path I enjoyed the mountain breeze and the richness of tranquility.

Having passed through a gorge so narrow that the sides almost touched, the mountain broadened out and a valley basin appeared. In some places, the river water spread and dispersed and as I stepped on an arrangement of stones in the water I realized that people had trodden this path before.

The path led me into an immense forest of chestnut trees and the roof of a thatched hut half appeared on the slope with a path leading to it. There were three interlinked ponds at the side of the path and the gate to the courtyard of the hut was made up of three planks of wood bound together with vines. A large rock stood by the gate and there was a toon tree by the house with a bird's nest built in its top. The roof was covered in thatch and the walls of the gate had been made from straw, a conical rain hat of straw hung on the wall. On a wooden tablet beneath the eaves was written in brushed characters: Zhongnan Ziwu Quanzhen'an—Quanzhen Temple (Temple of the Complete Truth) in the Ziwu valley of the Southern Hills.

There was no other sound here, just the noise of the water, the chattering of birds and the mountain wind. The air seemed to contain the scent of flowers. I pushed my staff into the ground by the fence and put down my knapsack in front of the hut.

A daoist emerged, said nothing but smiled, I felt as if I was bathed in the spring wind. He was the thinnest hermit that I had ever seen in the hills but his gaze was as bright as that of a child.

His gestures and expression welcomed me into the hut. The hut was extremely small. Through the entrance there was a very narrow kitchen, he took a bowlful of flour from an earthenware jar and began to knead dough. Further on there was a large *kang*—a   heated brick bed and I took off my

75

shoes and sat down on it. There was a place with a mosquito net in the room where the daoist slept and there were two small windows in the rear wall through which you could see the valley that I had climbed. In a corner, I discovered the only piece of furniture, a battered wooden chest. Written on a plank of the rear wall was: "Use straw and twigs of pine as fuel, eat the roots of wild herbs." No phrase could be a more appropriate footnote to this kind of thatched temple life.

I discovered a hardback notebook lying beside a tattered mat with holes in it. It contained some sentences which I copied into the pocket book that I carried with me:

> Where lies the harm
> In mutual visits of the uninvolved?
> Fear only the good and bad
> Of the spoken word.
>
> Of true joy and leisure
> Nothing can be said.
> Reach the infinite and sublime
> And do away with discussion.
>
> The spirit scatters
> At talk of right and wrong,
> And virtue is forgotten
> In falsities of fame and profit.
>
> Better the mind
> Limpid in silence
> That achieves mutual tranquility
> In nature.

▶ A hermit's poem (Photo/Guo Feng)

It was a poem by the Jin dynasty daoist, Ma Danyang (1123 – 1183), one of the seven disciples of the daoist Complete Truth School, whose daoist name was Danyangzi. Tradition has it that when very young he could write poetry and wrote a poem entitled *Riding the Clouds on a Crane*. Adults were curious as to why a child should think like this. He obtained a doctorate at the age of 20 and thereafter received a county level appointment in charge of the six sections that dealt with defense, investigation and punishment, building and engineering works, personnel and administration, lands and taxation, rites and ceremonies. However he had little interest in an official career, his ideal was to embrace the origin of things and abide by unity (*bao yuan shou yi*), to refine energy and practice the way. It is said that when drunk he once said to himself: "There's someone holding me up in my drunkenness."

In 1167 he met Wang Chongyang (1113 – 1170), the founder of the Complete Truth School who said to him: "I have come all this way to hold up the drunkard." Ma Danyang thereupon had a sudden moment of enlightenment and he and his wife Sun Bu'er, took Wang Chongyang as their principal teacher. He gave up his family property and practiced the way in the Kunlun Mountains. Ma Danyang was Wang Chongyang's first disciple in Shandong, he had seven disciples in all who were known as the "seven sons of the Complete Truth".

After the death of Wang Chongyang Ma Danyang continued the Complete Truth School and founded his own Yuxian Sect, taking in pupils and acquiring many disciples. Ordinarily, Ma Danyang preached the way, talked and laughed, happy and at ease in himself. One day, he suddenly said to his disciples: "Today there will be something to celebrate." Not long after, he suddenly passed away. The Chongyang palace where Ma Danyang was living at the time is in Hu county, off the mountain, some tens of kilometers from where I was.

In a short while, the daoist master came and sat on the *kang* and I started asking him questions. I put the questions and he replied in writing. He first wrote:

At the temple of the Complete Truth
I am no man of affairs.
Respect poverty and honor the way,
And dwell in detachment.

The mind does not obstruct
The overnight guest,
To roam at leisure
Wherever he wills.

I swiftly gave thanks, thinking to stay the night and to go down the mountain in the morning.

Q: Why has the master ceased to speak? What is the difference between speaking and not speaking?

A: In not speaking the uninvolved do not interfere with each other and come to a whole hearted and calm realization of the Classic of Purity and Tranquility. Excessive discussion of destiny is not better than the state of inaction that can bring many kinds of wonderful self knowledge.

Q: How do you practice?

A: Every day I eat and sleep. I rise with the birds and when they rest, I sleep. I sit when unoccupied and walk in leisure when there is time. Without involvement in affairs I am at peace with myself.

Q: What is the criterion for achieving the way?

A: I have not achieved the way, nor do I know it, I know only that each day is as it is and that is all.

Q: I have seen that in some large daoist temples there are many daoist masters who are busy and active all day, helping people set up home and divining the *fengshui*, is this practice too?

A: An ancient master once said: "Experience transforms man" (that is to say, the experience of the trials and tribulations of life and death acts ceaselessly to transforms people). The way has corpus and implementation: corpus means the way as it was undertaken by the early forefathers of the Complete Truth School, implementation is what you say and so on, they are expounded for all the people of the world.

Q: I've heard that in the Southern Hills there is a practicing daoist master who lives "with pine flowers overhead, dining on pine kernels and with river, pine and moon for company, drinking the wind in the pines", who eats only a pine cone or a pine needle a day. Do you know where he lives?

A: "In the practice of the way, the Southern Hills have the crown." The hills have been a village for the immortals since ancient times and have become so once more. There are hermits there who have become immortal, but as to where they are, if you have the affinity you may meet them.

Q: Why is it that in ancient times so many achieved enlightenment in the way, and in modern times there are so few?

A: In sorrow the ancient masters felt concern for all sentient beings, but because of our vain aspirations it is difficult to achieve a stable civilization. "Experience transforms man" is a natural principle of the way of the immortals, the calamity of mankind today is difficult to put right, thus those with sincerity may themselves know and understand.

Q: I have heard that more than 500 practitioners in the Southern Hills receive an allowance of 80 yuan a month through the generosity of a lay buddhist in Hong Kong, is this so?

A: That's for Buddhism, daoists haven't heard of it.

Q: Where does the support for your life come from?

A: Use surplus to make up insufficiency. I wander abroad with my bamboo staff. If I have nothing I sleep on the street. If I have money I put it to good causes. Hardship is a joy, there is good in bad times, there is nothing fixed.

Q: Don't you feel lonely living in the hills? When there's a festival in the bustling world below and you are here by yourself sitting in the moonlight, don't you find the days hard to bear?

As I asked my question, the daoist master's mood became remote and he gazed through the window at the blue mountains for a long time, picked up his brush and then wrote: "Neighboring nations can see each other, dogs and chickens can hear each other and people can live into old age without contact with each other." "Take delight in what you eat and wear, take joy in life and living." [1]

The occupant of the Quanzhen Temple was called Hou, he had been born in Hainan province and had grown up in Zhuhai and had been the general manager of a firm in Hainan before he came to the Southern Hills. As a child he had been puzzled by life and had not been able to explain it. He had studied *Qigong* and later abandoned it. He said that all that was an absurd fantasy and a vain accomplishment, it was not the ultimate.

He had become a daoist in 1989 at the Yuquan Temple on Mount Huashan where he had spent over ten years studying with a master and living the life of a daoist temple, he had then come here. He took me to see the hut that he had occupied when he first arrived.

---

1 These are two quotations from the *Daodejing* by Laozi. There are many translations into English and just as many expansions and interpretations of their meaning. This daoist master seems to take a particular view based on solitude rather than community. —*Trans*

▲ Daoist master Hou's straw hut (Photo/Guo Feng)

It was open to the air on all sides and it was different from other places in the wilderness in that it had an opening in the roof, it was an abandoned hill dweller's house. Later he had built his present hut with his own hands, its roof was covered with thatch held down by beams of wood secured to the ridge pole by vines. Underneath the thatch there was a sheet of plastic to keep the water out. The lean-to roof of the kitchen was formed from woven reeds, enough to let out steam but the mountain winds visited in the winter.

He had lived here without speaking for two years and he planned to stay here without speaking for ten years.

He said that there were daoist monks living in a cave on Wangdaoling on the slope opposite the eastern peak of Mount Huashan. I could try my luck and go and see whether I could meet them. I asked him who his master was. He told me that daoists had an inherited master pupil system, a unique tradition that the ordinary person did not know of. If you truly sought the way a master would come and find you, it was a matter of sincerity and sensitivity, the key lay in the kind of mind that you had. We concluded our paper conversation and looked up to see that it was time to eat.

Master Hou went to cook, he suggested that if I were interested I could go and look at the bird's nest beside the hut. The nest was built in the very middle of the tree, the tree trunk was not very thick. The mountain winds were strong and the nest swayed in the wind with the tree, watching it made you anxious.

When the food was ready we sat on a tree trunk and enjoyed the noodles. The noodles seemed made by a specialist but there was no salt in Master Hou's temple hut, I looked for the salt jar and found that there was not a grain left. Fortunately, there was some stir-fryed asparagus lettuce which Master Hou had just dug up and my appetite was good. Master Hou cooked me some more noodles and to my embarrassment I left some, I think I was too greedy.

After we had finished eating, Master Hou took me to look at the bird's nest. He said that the pica bird had spent six months unsuccessfully trying to build a nest but hadn't managed a single twig, it had tried all the twigs but without avail, possibly because there were too few branches on the tree and the branches themselves were extremely slippery, anywhere else and it would have been an easy. Why did it not go and build its nest in another tree? I guessed this was a secret between the bird and the daoist.

Finally, it had managed the first twig at New Year the previous year and the building work had been more or less completed in fifteen days. The nest was finished and there were chicks. Suddenly, a week before the earthquake, the bird began to rebuild and strengthen the nest.

During the afternoon, Master Hou sat meditating in the temple. There was a billhook in the yard and I dragged in several branches to practice the art of chopping firewood. Next to me was the large stone that blocked the entrance, the daoist, who had experience of chopping firewood, told me that the stone was called the "stone without a heart". He said that the stone had been moved down there a week before the earthquake. On level ground, three of them had been unable to shift it to the entrance. They had eventually gone down the mountain and returned after the earthquake to find that a crack had opened in the earth at the place where they had originally planned to put the stone, if it had been there, it would have fallen down. Do stones have hearts or not? He took me to see a crack caused by a 6.5 degree aftershock two days previously.

Thereafter I went to the vegetable patch with Master Hou to pull grass. The grass was growing as luxuriantly as the vegetables. Above the vegetable patch there were three ponds which provided drinking water. The ponds were a bit of a mixture, spring water seeped from the grass into the one at the top, the water was clear and you could see the bottom, there were no weeds round it nor any insects. The second pond was slightly lower and took the overflow directly from the first. There were some tadpoles in the second and even more in the third. I asked the daoist what the secret of the ponds was. He stirred up the first pond with a hoe and, in a while, the muddy water gradually cleared and returned to its original state. Master Hou said that the three ponds of spring water were like the human body—top (*shen*/soul), middle (*qi*/energy) and bottom (*jing*/essence)—three corporeal seats of daoist energy.

Like a bird, the sun folded the wings of its rays and darkness entered the gorge. Master Hou started to walk round the yard.

▲ A hermit's place of meditation (Photo/Zhang Jianfeng)

He waved his hands, raised his feet and stretched out his arms as if he were flying, or walking or dancing. His movements were elegant and I believed that he was performing an ancient form of shadow boxing.

Night fell and the human figure seemed to disappear into an inky blackness. There were no lamps lit inside the hut and I sat in the darkness listening to the singing of night birds while Master Hou sat in meditation. There was a constant gurgling noise of swallowing in his throat and as I listened I went to sleep.

The next morning I got up to the sound of all the birds on the mountain singing and thought that Master Hou had no need to rely on a clock, the birds could tell him the time.

I had always wondered why his mosquito net was so narrow. I didn't know how he slept but thinking of the previous night I suddenly realized that he passed every night in seated meditation.

Breakfast was a porridge of corn on the cob rice and sweet potatoes, the stove was connected to the *kang*, the wood smoke entering the *kang* and turning to heat.

Although I had always refused porridge, I finished off this helping and almost licked up the left-over grains remaining in the bowl.

After breakfast I tried on the rush raincoat and conical bamboo hat that were hanging on the back of the door, in them I looked like a counterfeit hermit.

Master Hou said that there was another daoist nearby who had taken a vow of silence, I followed his hand as he pointed out the direction, it was an eyeful of blue hills, apart from the passing breeze it was a sea of trees and I could see nothing. He suggested that it was better not to disturb him. I nodded vigorously and prepared to say goodbye.

Master Hou said that what one saw and heard in a day was not part of the way and should not be taken into account. One should be like a child and distinguish unconsciously, that was truth.

As I left he gave me a pair of straw sandals and exhorted me to tread on firm ground, step by step and glory would appear from beneath my feet.

I had a relaxed walk down the mountain and flew, like a rolling stone, from the depths of the gorge to its entrance. In the cluster of trees opposite there seemed to be a hut where somebody should be living in seclusion, but there was neither the sound of a voice nor any smoke.

I had never heard that there was anybody in seclusion there. It was opposite the gorge and the undergrowth was thick, the ravine was narrow and the river deep and as it flowed the water gave out the sound of emptiness. I searched for about an hour in the scrub and undergrowth and found no human or animal tracks and so returned to the stretch of path at the place where I had discovered the hut, mopping my perspiration with a sigh.

Back again at the stone bridge where the path had divided, I retraced my original path back. As I passed the place where I had bought the bamboo staff in Qiliping, a hill dweller urged me to rest my feet. I took a fancy to one of the staffs that he was selling, it was a natural dragon headed walking stick but another old person was vigorously selling her wares and despite my explanation that I could only use one, she finally succeeded in selling me hers. With two walking sticks I then took to the mountain path on four legs.

Chapter Four

Jiawutai
—Hills Rich in Hermits and Potatoes

Viewed from the plain, Jiawutai resembles a flower in blossom. Like Mount Huashan it is made up of huge blocks of granite formed about four billion years ago. During the Tang dynasty (618 – 907), Zongmi (780 - 841), the Fifth Patriarch of the Avatamsaka School of Chinese Buddhism, practiced on its peaks. He started in a cliff cave and later founded the Xingqing Temple. Below the main peak is the Poshan Temple where the Fifth Dalai Lama (1617 – 1682) stayed during the Qing Dynasty. Later Yinguang, Xiuyun and Gao Henian (1872 – 1962) all stayed there briefly. It was destroyed during the Cultural Revolution, but several years ago the buddhist nun Nengren (1928 – 1997) rebuilt a bodhimanda there. When she died, her body remained whole and has now been encased in gold to receive the respect of worshippers.

The other peak of Jiawutai is called Mount Xuewashan (Snow Tile Mountain). It stands alongside the main peak and looks like two huge dragons soaring southwards. Past the Xingqing Temple are the dragon's back and dragon's spine. The temple is built on the dragon's back and the dragon's spine is less than a foot wide. Beyond the dragon's spine is the dragon's mouth, they join Mount Guanyin to the south. Mount Guanyin is shaped like a dragon's pearl and the Guanyin cave is the most mysterious place on the whole of Jiawutai. Mount

▲ Jiawutai in the clouds (Photo/Guo Feng)

Taixingshan, with the Cave of a Thousand Buddhas and the Cave of a Hundred Spirits, is to the east of Jiawutai.

Yitianmen Gate is a place name, its main marker is the Wuliangdian (Hall of the Immeasurable) Hut on the only path up the mountain, the hut where Zen Master Luo Gui lives. On my first visit to Jiawutai I passed it and didn't go in because it looked rather like an ancient village temple. Yitianmen Gate is the first entrance portal to Jiawutai and several huge stones stand at the entrance to Master Luo's hut. I went in, Master Luo Gui was working so I sat under the awning that had just been put up in the courtyard. Master Luo looked about fifty or sixty and had lived here for about eight years.

Very soon the woman who sold noodles under the entrance awning arrived bearing tea, she was a convert of Master Luo

Gui's and, with the simplicity of the countrywoman, kept topping up my tea, standing on one side almost forgetful of her own business.

Master Luo Gui said that he had only just put up the awning, tied to a tree to keep off the sun, with a table underneath that would seat eight tea drinkers so that people going down the mountain would have somewhere to cool off.

He had even more ideas, in several years time there might be an old people's center for practitioners here, a center for elderly practitioners in ill health who could no longer live in the hills, or lay practitioners at home who had nobody to look after them, or even elderly people without any social support. He had been busy on this for several years, the land certificate had now arrived and because of this he had learned how to get on with all shades of officialdom.

So far as living in the hills was concerned, Master Luo Gui said that practitioners did not live there on account of the circumstances, living in the hills was not for gilding their image, in fact there was not much difference between living in the hills and living in a monastery, the crux of the matter was how you perceived it. In truth, one could practice anywhere, he lived here out of affinity, the relationship was like the famous Zen koan: The wind blows, the flag moves, is it that the wind moves? Or the flag moves? Or is it the mind that moves?

Master Luo Gui recounted a story about a buddhist hermit monk in the Southern Hills.

Several years previously a lay practitioner had arrived from the far-off Northeast. He had come because he had heard someone in Beijing say that he had met three hermit monks in Jiawutai in the Southern Hills, one was 170 years old, one 240, and one over 400 years old. He had hurriedly bought a ticket to Xi'an but before he set out a stranger had sought out the practitioner and urged him to abandon his plan but he paid him no attention. Before departure, the train he had originally intended to take was derailed so he took another and arrived in Xi'an weary and travel stained.

En route, he enquired about the Southern Hills and, as directed, he had found a monk at the Jingye Temple and learned from him that there really were hermit monks in the Southern Hills. Subsequently, he had arrived at this hut at the entrance to Jiawutai, had left his luggage with Master Luo Gui and set off into the mountains where all he saw was the wind and the ever-changing clouds.

In the course of his search he had a meal of stewed mushrooms with several masters living in the hills and suffered mild food-poisoning. The three masters who had eaten with him were unlucky, they were severely poisoned and spent a long time in hospital at a cost of several tens of thousands of yuan, all raised by Master Luo Gui from buddhist lay people.

It is said that that mushroom stew was delicious in the extreme and they had picked a whole pailful of mushrooms. In general, they rarely met and it was not known what had brought them together to enjoy the mushrooms—though it seems that the mushrooms themselves harbored no ill intentions. Hill dwellers are well able to identify poisonous mushrooms. Master Dadao who lived at Liangshuiquan Spring (Cool Water Spring) above them had warned them not to eat the mushrooms. Some say that Master Dadao had eaten them as well, but he had magical powers.

Several years previously when Master Luo Gui had been meditating on a rock at the top of Mount Xuewashan, he had seen an old monk with a long beard on the precipice opposite. Later, he had gone across several times to search him out but had found no trace. All there had been was a small terrace big enough for a bird and above, a huge pine tree growing like a canopy over the precipice as the clouds billowed below. There was no cooking smoke in the surrounding area, even less any trace of humanity.

Many years ago somebody on Mount Dabaoshan opposite Jiawutai saw a forest of extraordinarily beautiful pagodas on the rear slope of Jiawutai. Everybody who lived on the mountain knew that there were no such buddhist pagodas on the rear slope.

During the Republic, Monk Elder Xuyun lived at the Shizi Maopeng (Lion Hut) on the rear slope and had seen Bodhisattvas without number in the Southern Hills. Fomianshan (Mountain of the Buddha Face) which was the very image of an upturned human face lay to the west of Jiawutai and it was said that seven buddhas lived there.

Master Yanli who lived up the mountain came down in the middle of the day and called into the Wuliangdian Hut for a rest on his way down. Master Yanli, Master Luo Gui and I sat drinking tea, the refreshments were chestnuts bought from the hill people. Master Yanli had lived in the mountains for over ten years in a hut in the depths of a gorge from where he could see the huts at the very top of the mountain.

The lay person who kept the stall outside served Master Yanli and I two large bowls of *liangpi* noodles. Although I was already full I could not resist the temptation of the *liangpi* topped with vegetables. Master Yanli refused to eat anything, he had stomach trouble and eat nothing at all, it saved trouble and he wanted to starve the sickness out. He said that if you put the concepts of body and illness out of your mind, they couldn't do anything to you. By the time I had lifted my head from the bowl, Master Yanli had already gone up the mountain. I said goodbye to Master Luo Gui and hastened after him, intending to go up the mountain with him.

▶ The mountain path to Jiawutai (Photo/Zhang Jianfeng)

He walked very fast and I rushed along on the paved path in pursuit a long way behind, I finally caught up with him at a stream where the valley took a turn.

Liangshuiquan Spring is in the upper reaches of the Yitianmen valley. It flows past the side of the hall of Master Yanli's hut day and night, the spring water rippling with coolness in the summer. The mountain path passes through the hut courtyard and continues beyond the back gate beside the stream.

The hut comprises a two storied hill dwelling and three large halls and had been a village temple in the past. Master Yanli had previously lived in Fucanggu, on the opposite hill. The village people had built the temple and had invited him to come and look after it. There is a temple fair on a fixed day every year when villagers from off mountain fill the two storied building in the courtyard. It was empty at the moment, there were no windows to the wooden floored upper story and it seemed rather ancient in date.

Master Yanli's sleeping place was partitioned off by planks and a curtain, there was no door and I didn't know how he managed in winter when the valley was snowbound. He had already lived here for five years, if there came a day when the hill dwellers would no longer let him live here he would go somewhere else.

After he had come into contact with Buddhism over ten years ago and become a buddhist he had studied for five years at the Wuming Buddhist College in Tibet, where he had to eat meat. In Tibet there had only been beef, mutton and cheese. Vegetables were available in distant towns but it meant a long journey to buy them. Vegetables and other foodstuffs were more expensive than meat and, in any case, vegetables very quickly froze into lumps of ice. He later left because of ill health and moved to Mount Wutaishan, north of the Southern

Hills where he had lived for a while. In Tibet he had burnt off the index finger of his left hand as a sacrifice to the Buddha, he said he had seen others do it and so he had done so too. It hadn't hurt too much, it had seemed already numb when it burned. Buddhism was fine, others were prepared to sacrifice their lives for their religion, he wasn't up to sacrificing his life but what was the sacrifice of a finger? The body of flesh was merely a false illusion.

He was a man who loved to laugh and laughed more than he spoke, his descriptions were often interrupted by laughter. He spoke crisply and clearly and with a sense of reality, his laughter echoing in the air and mingling with the sound of the spring water from the courtyard.

As it was getting dark he cooked noodles and brought me some, they were too much for me and I could hardly breathe as I eat them.

After the evening meal we sat cross legged on the steps of the large hall, I took his coir mat and Master Yanli squatted on a bench. The stars came out, the evening breeze settled over the hall, and the leaves on the trees rose and fell like a tide. Master Yanli put on the red Tibetan robe that he had brought back with him and I wrapped myself in a quilt. Master Yanli said that normally he slept sitting fully clothed on the steps at night. Sitting there on a winter' night he could clearly hear people talking over a distance of several *li*.

I asked Master Yanli why it was that people felt so stressed when the modern material world was so highly developed. He explained that it was because mankind was surrounded by matter that was not natural and was not naturally grown. Houses for example, the ancients had used only stone and wood but now they were all constructed of man-made synthetic materials.

As to life and death, he said that in the face of death people

were always filled with a formless dread but there was, in fact, nothing to be frightened of. Children were afraid of injections but there was nothing particularly frightening about injections, you wanted children not to be frightened of injections but that wasn't possible, it was one's mind playing tricks. Death was like a room in darkness, if you were familiar with its layout you weren't frightened. The principle of life and death was to overcome one's own fear of death.

There was too much that could be seen in this valley, especially in the winter but he was unwilling to say more.

In winter, snow sealed in the mountains, not a soul was to be seen and snow besieged the hut too. The hill dwellers sit in meditation in the company of their own shadows, listening to the sound of their own breathing. Snow falls outside and the mountains become even more emptily mysterious causing everything to lose direction. But at night one can distinctly hear people talking or somebody coming to knock at the entrance.

Years ago, when he had been living in the Wuhuadong Cave and the mountain had been similarly sealed off by snow, he had been meditating in the cave and had heard movement outside, the sound of footsteps approaching from a distance. His mind was filled with the fantastic idea that in such snow animals would also wish to shelter from the blizzard and if they came into the cave it would interfere with his meditation. However, there was a smaller cave on the path alongside which they could use for shelter. Just as he was thinking this, the creature outside seemed to pick up his thought and altered course to the smaller cave. The next morning, when the wind had dropped and it had stopped snowing, there were footprints as large as plates in front of the entrance, the distance between prints was over a meter. He did not know what animal it could

◀ A single plank bridge in the Southern Hills (Photo/Zhang Jianfeng)

have been at such a height on the mountain.

Master Yanli told us the story of the monk Miaoshan who once, living in a hut, was suddenly overcome by a desire to eat noodles, at that moment a girl appeared and presented him with a dish of noodles. Practitioners are accustomed to saying a grace and making an offering for homeless souls before a meal, at that point the girl suddenly made off and the noodles turned into insects.

There was also a Zen master who lived in a hut in the Southern Hills who was frequently visited by strangers at night. Elder Monk Xuyun presented him with a buddhist disciplinary stave and taught him its secret art. The Zen master hid it under the mat. Somebody came to visit at night and as usual the practitioner repeatedly asked: are you a convert to the Buddhist Trinity? The visitor immediately turned into a python, the Zen master struck out with the stave which flew and lodged in the python's stomach, spinning and emitting light. The python died in the valley. The Zen master recovered the stave from the python's belly and after washing it discovered that it had been dyed black by poison.

Living in the hills often leads to accidental obsessions where the practitioner is unable to free himself from a particular mental state. Some years ago there had been a *shami*, a buddhist novice living in this cave who frequently laughed and talked to himself. Later he suddenly became deranged whilst travelling and had to be hospitalized off mountain.

There is an extensive psychological ambience to the hills which, during meditation, can set off latent traits and impurities of the mind and present obstacles to the practitioner. This is one of the diseases of Zen. People who lack will and perseverance can be brought to this state which can lead to mental confusion and eventual derangement.

The darkness lightened in front of our eyes and after a

night of storytelling Master Yanli was tired and dozed with his head resting on the sutra covered desk at the bottom of the steps. I drowsed wrapped in my quilt and before I dropped off to sleep I saw from my watch that it was four o'clock in the morning, it would soon be dawn.

Next morning I woke to the sound of birds and Master Yanli had already gone to make breakfast. He pointed out a three foot long gap in the eaves where there was a large python, a common neighbor for both him and Master Dadao who lived close by. The python was always in the eaves and had once exposed a tail the thickness of an arm when on the roof beams of Master Dadao's hut next door. Master Yanli estimated that it could be over ten feet long. Once, when he had been reading under the eaves it had blown loudly through a crevice over the desk, like the breathing of somebody aggrieved, but it had never been willing to show itself fully.

Because he normally hardly ever slept in it he kept a knapsack on the bed in the hut. One day he discovered the empty knapsack suddenly bulging and making a *zhi zhi* sound, a small snake had made its home inside.

After breakfast with Master Yanli I went next door to the hut of Master Dadao. He was in the midst of eating. This was the second time that I had met him. On the previous occasion I had passed through his hut on my way up the mountain and had stopped there for a while.

Apart from the eighty or more year old nun Mother Changhua living in Ping'an Maopeng (Peace Hut), he had lived on the front of the mountain longer than anybody and had been there for more than 20 years. Many of the old practitioners who had lived on the mountain after the Cultural Revolution had already passed away and many of the masters who had come up the mountain after the Cultural Revolution had moved to the large monasteries in the south.

During the years when *Qigong* was fashionable, Master Dadao had been widely known for his supernatural powers and for curing sickness through *Qigong*. His actual status was that of a lay person. He was in his sixties, alone in the world and had not yet achieved an affinity suitable for taking his vows. His family home was in a little village off the mountain not far away. When young he had liked to be in the company of daoists and buddhist monks and even earlier he had studied Buddhism at the Wuzhen Temple off the mountain, later staying at the Xingjiao Temple and Mount Taixingshan. In 1982 he had gone to the top of the mountain and lived as a monk with Monk Jicheng, the abbot of the Xingqing Temple.

Because he had not taken vows, he had come down from the mountain top after Monk Jicheng's death. He had lived in very many of the huts on the mountain and was familiar with all the local conditions.

I had heard from other hill dwellers that Master Dadao possessed magical powers and asked him about them, he said it was all rumor.

He had lived in these mountains for many years and had never slept at night. He said that there was much that could be seen at night, things on and off mountain and astronomical events appearing one after the other.

He had a very pessimistic view about the state of society and social developments and said that the survival of mankind had never been in more danger than it was today. Mankind had brought upon itself the threats to its existence. They were far greater than earthquakes, volcanoes, storms, floods, drought and viruses. This was a response to the failure of mankind to move towards virtue. Who was there in the world who did not seek advantage? If you sought advantage then your motivation and objectives would certainly harm others to the profit of oneself. How could there be harmony in the world, if everybody harmed others for their own profit? People were only aware of instant enjoyment and not of the dangers that stared them in the face. If the heart was honest, there would be fine weather and all would be well. If man was not inclined towards virtue and lacked compassion then the gods themselves could not save him.

After eating, Master Dadao willingly took me up the mountain for a walk. Liangshuiquan Spring lay in the valley surrounded by mountains; as you climbed the mountain and looked down from the ridge, the peaks surrounded you like a lotus. From the heights you could see the huts of Masters Yanli and Dadao nestled amongst the lotus flowers.

The first high point on the ridge was dragon's leap, from whence you descended two *li* to Erlongdong Cave (Second Dragon Cave) where a Zen master lived. From thereon upwards there was a ladder surrounded on three sides by a precipice. The stairs extended upwards for over 30 meters with an iron chain that could be grasped on either side. Having climbed the ladder you entered a small cave entrance built from rock, above it was a huge rock with three halls built of wood and clay dedicated to the Ksitigarbha Buddha. At its foot, in front of the halls was a courtyard a few meters square surrounded on three sides by a precipice. The path passed beneath the rock.

I sat resting on the steps of the hall with Master Dadao as the mountain breeze dried the sweat on our faces.

Master Yinchao was lighting the fire to cook in an eating area built from fencing and the Ksitigarbha Buddha sat upright in his hall. The scenery was marvelous but unfortunately the roof above the Buddha let in the light and perhaps the Buddha needed a rain hat. If it rained heavily there would be a shower in the hall. Apart from the statue of the Buddha and ten statues of Yanwang, the king of the underworld, I could see nothing else.

Master Yinchao was a southerner who had become a buddhist over ten years earlier and had visited the four great buddhist mountains, he had carried a stick of incense and performed a *ke tou* prostration every three paces.

He was an excitable man who spoke very fast. His little dining hall looked as if it had been built not long ago, the walls were of plaited twig fence panels plastered with mud. How could he sleep there at night? I could see nowhere else that he could sleep. Apart from the three halls and the dining place beneath the eaves there was no other structure.

Master Yinchao was too hospitable and busily called me to have a drink. The dining area was under the eaves of the Ksitigarbha Buddha's hall and was rain-proof at a pinch. The sun was fierce in the middle of the day, the smoke could not escape from the dining area and it brought tears to his eyes. He was cooking fried rice and had made pumpkin soup.

We sat on the hall steps looking at the distant scenery below the mountain as we eat. The rice was excellent and the pumpkin soup tasted very good. At every mouthful of soup Master Yinchao heaped praise on his own culinary skills and the flavor of the pumpkin soup. Because of its height above sea level there was a shortage of water. There were no large trees at the top of the mountain, there was less than ten square meters of level ground within the courtyard and the water supply came from rainwater, firewood had to be collected from down the mountain.

After a short rest we continued upwards. Poshan Temple was above the Ksitigarbha Halls and was built in between several large rocks. At the mountain entrance beside the precipice there was a large rock split into a narrow gap through which the path passed, legend has it that Emperor Guansheng carved out the path with a knife.

The entrance to the Poshan Temple is built up against an

enormous rock and there is a precipice not three feet from the entrance. A large rock divides the courtyard into front and rear courts. There is a single cell in the front court and three cells and two dining areas in the rear court, together with the three halls. An inscription in the temple records the year of construction as 627.

A small path cut into the cliff face by the rear court leads to the lama cave where the Fifth Dalai Lama lived for a while at the end of the Ming dynasty (1368 – 1644). Dadao said that a few years previously a nun had moved into the cave intending to stay there for some time but had only stayed one night and then moved down the mountain. Somebody had entered the cave and spoken to her during the night and scared her away. The cave was on the very edge of a precipice, nobody could get in once the door was closed.

It was already late when I arrived at the Ksitigarbha Hall and Master Yinchao gave me the half of a pumpkin that he had grown, a present for spending the night at the Poshan Temple.

That night, Master Yifa installed me in the monk's quarters in the lama cave in the rear court. We sat crossed legged on mats. The stars in the night sky shone like lotus blossom and dazzled the eyes with their tranquil purity. I wanted to sleep out under the stars but the wind was quite strong and the night was cold.

Master Yifa had arrived here in the winter of the previous year. He had used to live in the south. He said that he did not know how he had managed to survive that bitterest winter in a hundred years, but he had. The winds in the hills had been particularly high, there had been no time to install a heated brick bed as there was very little firewood in the hills. I asked no further.

The eastern wall of the courtyard had collapsed and had not been rebuilt. The back wall of the hall in the rear courtyard had also fallen down. The halls' foundations dated from the Tang dynasty and were beginning to collapse outwards. The only path up the mountain ran below the foundations and below the path was a precipice. Master Yifa sighed, he didn't know when it might collapse and people might be crushed to death and he didn't know when he might come across an opportune visitor. He said that he now felt that he no longer had the ability to carry out repairs here nor could he beg. In the south, such an ancient temple would have been rebuilt long ago. But it was no good here, repairing a temple had to wait on pre-destiny. He longed for it to be repaired at his hands but if there was insufficient affinity he would continue to look after it until someone came and took over from him.

He was already planning to clear away the shattered stone from beneath the large rocks but this required a stone crusher and the hire of labor, using the crushed stone on the spot to build up the eastern wall and finally demolishing and rebuilding the hall in the rear courtyard. We reckoned that the overall budget would amount to about 70,000 yuan. This was no small sum.

He intended to take the opportunity of his presence here to hand on the best of what he had built to a successor. If somebody suitable could take over he would leave and go somewhere else.

My luggage was in the monk's quarters in the rear courtyard opposite, and that night I would be sleeping there by myself.

Master Yifa was sitting opposite me, I saw red light as if from a lamp suddenly appear in the room behind him and flash three times. There was no source of light in the room at all, where had the light come from? Behind the room was a precipice and beneath the precipice the valley. The mountains opposite were some distance away with no sign of people.

When I rose in the morning I followed the little path along the precipice to look at the lama cave, Master Yifa was sitting meditating by the large rock outside the entrance with a sea of cloud in front of him. The valley was invisible, it was a sea in which waves of cloud rose and fell, the mountains opposite had also sunk beneath the waves. The sun rose in the east and seemed to make a rolling sound.

After he had finished meditation Master Yifa began to make a breakfast of millet porridge and wild herbs.

After breakfast he taught me dynamic Zen meditation. He crossed his arms, steadied his expression and moved back and forth in the narrow courtyard, the wide sleeves of his robe dancing in the wind as if about to take flight.

He said that when you move in a relaxed way, you just have to feel that you are moving for it to be effective. As you slowly experience it you come to know the joy of movement. There is nothing in the mind but the pacing of your feet. With the wind beneath them, your feet become lighter and your body less clumsy and more at ease. There is nothing else, just a sense of gradual realization. Zen lies in that moment of relaxed movement.

The early morning sun shone from the east of the temple into the courtyard through the gap in the surrounding wall, and in the yellow iridescent sunlight we walked our own paths back and forth, Master Yifa on one side and myself on the other, heads lowered in silence, brushing shoulders as we passed.

Master Yinchao came up from the Ksitigarbha Hall at noon to enquire how I had slept but didn't stay and went down again.

That was a week ago. A padlock now hangs on the great door of the Poshan Temple. We went up to the rocky outcrop above the temple, Dadao wanted to visit his master the monk Jicheng whose stupa was amongst the trees on the summit. Looking down we could see a figure in the courtyard of the

Poshan Temple. Master Dadao said that it ought to be Master Yifa, strangely he had locked himself into the temple and I thought, perhaps, that he hoped not to be disturbed.

The Xingqing Temple at the summit of Jiawutai lay above Jicheng's stupa, a building with five courts had stood here and the site of Jicheng's stupa was its former entrance, you now climbed the stone stairway from below.

The Xingqing Temple had been miraculously built by the Tang dynasty Zen Master Zongmi. It is said that at the time, the glazed tiles had been piled on the top of Mount Xuewashan and thrown across from the opposite peak. The bricks had come up with a train of pack-goats.

During the Cultural Revolution, Red Guards had braved the steep mountain and climbed up here, the thousand year old temple had been unable to resist their fists and feet, when they departed nothing had been left standing on the great terrace.

About 30 years ago Jicheng arrived here from Beijing and started rebuilding this bodhimanda. It is said that while he was living on the mountain a large number of local officials subscribed to the maintenance of buddhist buildings and every year buddhist services were held here attended by crowds of people from the towns and villages off mountain. Tractors had hauled supplies up the mountain and it is said that this long narrow mountain top had accommodated over 10,000 pilgrims.

At present there is a moss-covered cave entrance beneath the gateway, at the time it was a passage through to the underground level of the great building but it is now abandoned.

The American sinologist Bill Porter visited here over ten years ago when the monk Jicheng was still alive. At that time the path passed through the temple courtyard and then under a large rock behind the courtyard where there is a small gazebo constructed of earth and wood. When you emerge from the temple, Shenxianchang (the Place of the Immortals) and dragon ridge lie before you.

Later on, Master Huijian sealed off the back door on to the mountain with piles of firewood and built a new plank road across the eastern cliff face with cement boarding.

The entrance to the Xingqing Temple now stands in isolation, a precipice to the left and right of the courtyard saving the need for a surrounding wall.

At noon, Dadao knocked at the great door of the Xingqing Temple and Muxian, the only master who lived here permanently, came to open it.

Behind the statues of the Buddha in the great hall there is a side door that gives on to the rear courtyard of the temple. The wooden structures of the temple could accommodate not a few monks but the rear hall was locked. This was the time of Master Muxian's mid-day meal but neither Dadao nor I wanted to eat. We sat drinking the Iron Buddha tea that he had made with rain water and watched him eat. He sat cross-legged on a coir mat eating with fragrant enjoyment. He was eating noodles and the crisp sound as he chewed on the dark green vegetables was like an elegant accompaniment, he turned eating a simple meal like this one into a message.

Master Muxian said you see me eating very simply but very well, there's no lack of nourishment and I grow my own vegetables. I am at ease and free here, my wants are few, I need only the minimum of supplies each month, I have no surplus belongings and nothing on my mind. I eat, meditate, read the sutras and sleep. This is the entirety of my life.

Because he had planted an inexhaustible supply of vegetables, the day was nearly wholly devoted to the business of eating. Living a life in the mountains required spending a great deal of time on food, supplies had to be carried up the

mountain, and much time had to be spent in actually cooking.

The major problem was that it was easy to become slack because of not getting up in the morning and sleeping too well. He was fresh-faced and seemed about thirty years old.

Some ten years previously he had left home for the Gaomin Temple at Yangzhou where he had practiced for several years and had gone from there to the Wuming Buddhist College in Sertar county in Tibet. The college is currently reputed to have the best buddhist education in the world. Whilst there he had chanced upon the ascent to paradise of a person of accomplishment and had seen the unimaginable sight of the phenomenon of a heavenly shower of post-cremation crystals. To start with the crystals had been like rain and he had been unable to catch any but in the end had collected just eight crystals. After that, he had come here.

He said that everything was pre-destined, a buddhist lived here today and maybe somewhere else tomorrow. Although this place was very dilapidated he could not deliberately set about repairing it. As far as practice was concerned living in one place was as good as another, he just wanted to spend more time on practice, if destiny came to fruition then naturally someone would come and do the repairs, it was not something to be sought out intentionally.

Over the last few years he had appeared in all sorts of different places and normally he was not in touch with his family. He felt that the way he now lived was not bad, if he had not become a buddhist, his parents would have had to spend money on his wedding in their old age, buy a house and then look after the children. He was fine at the moment and at the least he was no burden on them. When they perhaps

◀ Masters Dadao and Muxian meet behind the Xingqing Temple (Photo/Zhang Jianfeng)

forgot that they had this son of theirs, they might unexpectedly receive news of him.

In fact, the demands of parents upon children were very few. All they hoped for was your well-being. Friends and relatives would all leave this world sooner or later and he had merely left his parents a little earlier. He said that if you wanted to leave the mundane world it should be as soon as possible. If you go, in six months or a year, your girlfriend will find somebody suitable. They won't stop living just because of you.

Of course, if you do leave it's best to find an unfamiliar place that they don't know of and restart your life there. Have you heard the saying: Life is a dream and death an episode in the dream. In the dream there are riches and honor but you wake to poverty. To dream everyday but not realize its futility is to dream in vain.

There were high winds here even though the sun was overhead. The roof of the temple had once been covered with iron tiles, which were now piled in a corner of the courtyard. Master Muxian took me to look behind the hall. In a corner there was a wooden door on what used to be the only way up the mountain and if you looked out you could see the blue of Mount Xuewashan opposite and the great rocks of the dragon's head.

Behind the great hall, the ground widened out and although it was on a slope, the presence of two large rocks made it an ideal place for seated meditation.

The face of the rock bore mottled and indistinct inscriptions, traces left by the daoists of the Tang and Song dynasties. Below the rocks ran the path, now overgrown with grass, that emerged from the gate through the gazebo towards dragon ridge.

After returning to the rear court and drinking his fill of tea, Master Dadao said goodbye to us and returned to his hut in the depths of the gorge. I sat and continued drinking tea.

As the sun sank towards the west I said goodbye to Master Muxian and made my way towards dragon's mouth. Once out of the entrance of the great hall, I started down through the side entrance of the Xingqing Temple where there was no surrounding wall and where the cliff face path, suspended over emptiness, went up over dragon ridge and then wound its way down westwards.

Jiawutai is a huge stone dragon and the way the huts at dragon's mouth were built was beyond comprehension, a vast stone rampart extended several tens of meters into the emptiness beneath the open mouth of the dragon and the two yellow mud huts were squeezed in under this stone wall. Below the cliff wall of the huts lay an abyss of ever-changing cloud.

Several day-lilies were planted outside the fence at the entrance to the huts.

I thought that the occupant here was someone who liked reading and perhaps had a deep feeling for the *Book of Songs*. I approached the fence and recited one of the names of the Buddha and the occupant came out, greeted me, opened the gate and let me in. His buddhist name was Yijing, he was in his thirties, fresh-faced and seemed in good shape. Of all the practitioners I had seen in these heights he seemed most to have the air of a scholar.

The hut just contained a bed, a niche for a statue, a small table and a shelf of books. There was no surplus space. The eating space was even smaller. I didn't see any water cistern and the master told me that each time he went down the mountain to fetch water he carried up 30 kilos weight of it on his back which lasted him a month. A trip to the river and back took over three hours.

He produced two packets of instant noodles for me to eat. He said the he eat one meal a day, he took things as they came, he didn't much care what he eat, the most basic requirements

111

▲ A distant view of the dragon's mouth on Jiawutai from Mount Xuewashan (Photo/Guo Feng)

to maintain health were sufficient and in any case too much food made you mentally lethargic. He was unwilling to spend more time on these sort of things. He said that Master Benxu's disciple at the Shizi Maopeng on the rear slope of the mountain was very good at making *jiaozi*[1] which they eat frequently, if I was lucky I might eat them if I went over there.

It had taken him two years to conquer his mental lethargy. For two years he had slept on a log, any lethargy and the

---

1 A kind of ravioli; in this case of finely chopped herbs or vegetables contained in a half moon shaped noodle skin.—*Trans*

▲ Longkou Maopeng (the Dragon's Mouth Hut) (Photo/Guo Feng)

moment he moved he would fall off, when he woke he would continue meditating, later he gradually overcame the lethargy.

After one has found one's true self, there is no difference between sleeping and waking. Whilst asleep one can see everything that is around you. Once having overcome lethargy it is possible to become gradually more mentally alert day by day and with the spirit full there is no desire to sleep. After the body has been purified there is no sleep, it is only the body that slumbers, the mind is clear.

Buddhism divides sleep into twelve sub-divisions. Lethargy the deep and sleep the shallow. Lethargy occupies the space between right and wrong, heavy lethargy is like grasping at floating shadows and mild lethargy like watching a film.

More than ten years earlier he had become a buddhist at the Gaomin Temple, the temple with the highest concentration of senior Zen monks in China in modern times and which still maintained a reputation for buddhist sanctity. Subsequently he had received instruction from the monk elders Xuyun and Laiguo. A few years ago at Mount Wutaishan, the monk elder Huitong (1927 – 2012) had directed him to come and live in a hut in the Southern Hills.

Master Yijing said that it was not easy to live in the hills. An ancient practitioner had said that one could not live in the hills without enlightenment. It was the only way to ward off day-long fantasies and to avoid being scared away by the conditions.

As you look to the south from the entrance of the Longkou Maopeng (the Dragon's Mouth Hut), the nearest mountain is the peak of the Guanyin Cave. To the west are the heights of Mount Xuewashan where there is the head of another dragon. After climbing to the peak of the Guanyin Cave to take a photograph of the Longkou Maopeng, I started down the valley and passing through undergrowth where others seem to have trodden before, climbed out on to the path towards Mount Xuewashan.

You needed the agility of an ape to climb this path, which lay amongst the broken rock of the mountain and was covered in fallen leaves. I didn't know how long it had been since anybody had been through here. On one side of the path there was an abyss, in some places there was a rusty iron chain as a handgrip. At the summit of the mountain a hut faced west beneath two large rocks, its roof lavishly tiled in red, its entrance was open, there was a rusty chime and a broken iron pot lay close by.

The courtyard was filled with orchids and a deep narrow gulley ran round the hut. The gulley was formed by the crack between two giant stones where there was a pool with gleaming white rocks. The surface of the giant stones was flat and I very much wanted to go to sleep on it. There was a cave beneath this platform containing a statue.

There was a ravine on three sides of the platform and the wind blew in from all three sides. There was not a speck of dirt on the surface of the rock and it was actually cleaner than my clothes. I went up and sat there, my shadow stamped on it. The blue green of the mountains opposite looked like a transparent landscape painting, its water vapor gently drifting in front of the eyes, I wanted to imprint it on my soul and carry it away.

An elderly monk sat meditating beside me and in the cave a fire burned with the color of plum blossom. I was surrounded by the spring grass, the summer rain, the autumn clouds and the winter snow. In the wind, the trees stood in the calm of Zen and the stones knocked on the dried grass like a wooden fish clapper. I didn't know how long I sat there and when I stood up, for a moment I did not know where I had come from or where I was going.

As I looked around, everything seemed to have changed to the color of gold, and a lotus shaped cloud floated behind the Longkou Maopeng. I made several attempts to catch it in the focus of my camera but without success. I then began to withdraw back down the mountain bit by bit, walking on this kind of mountain path is real walking, reciting step by step and if you miss a step you may lose your foothold and tumble. However, following the way of Daoism is a great deal more dangerous than this.

At the bottom of the mountain, covered in wind-blown sweat, I felt that my body had been completely colored by the wind. It was now summer but if it was autumn I might be fire-red.

Beneath the ochre sky, the scenery of the hills seemed carved in stone and I hurried to find somewhere to stay the night. Thinking it over, I decided that there was probably room at the Xingqing Temple and so returned there and knocked at the entrance as night was falling.

After meditating, I chanted a sutra by the light of a candle provided by Master Muxian and then fell asleep. The rats in the rafters seemed not to have come across a stranger for some time, they were very excited and danced the night through up above, sometimes with vocal accompaniment. I took little notice, nobody could haul me from my bed.

After watching the sun rise next morning, I sat in the eating area and took up the bellows, the flames in the fireplace looked like plum blossom in the snow and sparks as white as snowflakes filled the air and settled on my eyebrows.

It was 1,800 meters above sea-level and difficult to boil water so that eating was not easy. Master Muxian was in the kitchen with a ladle and I was soon eating snow white noodles with the dark green vegetables that he had grown himself.

After breakfast I took up the staff that he had given me and set out on the path towards the Guanyin Cave.

The Guanyin Cave was set above a precipice and its entrance, like a cleft in the rock that would only take one person at a time, was on a platform that jutted out in to thin air; the windows opened over a south-facing cliff face, opposite were blue-green mountain peaks and sometimes white clouds hung above them like curtains, changing shape all the time. If you wanted to get here without a guide you would only discover it from the air.

Last time, when I had stood in the fog at the entrance to the cave reciting the names of the Buddha, nobody had come for a long time, although there seemed to be somebody inside gathering vegetables. I had eventually left. This time, in order to test my patience I continuously recited the titles of the Amitabha Buddha, thinking that if the hermit was unwilling to open the door it would be a loss of face for the Amitabha Buddha. This time the door was opened.

The nun who opened the door said that I was fortunate, generally people left if those within paid no attention. I was an exception. At that moment the sun shone across from above the peak opposite and the rock above the cave seemed to open naturally, a ray of light entered and the wall of stone became a brilliant gold. Once through the red cave entrance, the width of a person, there was an eating area and then it suddenly narrowed. There was a buddha hall below the platform with a stone window through which the sun was shining, bathing the statue niche in light.

Two nuns lived in the cave, the master and her disciple, it was the disciple who had opened the door to me, neither of them would tell me their buddhist names. The older nun said that some years previously she had visited all the famous mountains. If doors weren't opened they just waited them out. That was the trick of it, she chuckled. If you hadn't waited as long you did, you wouldn't have got into this cave today. Sometimes we close the door when we see people coming, we pull a long face but there's actually nothing on our mind. Some people are just thirsty and want a drink, we cannot refuse them.

She said that the fact that I had got in today was a matter of destiny. My luck was in and I was just in time to eat *jiaozi*, they would be ready instantly. Hill dwellers did not often eat *jiaozi*, I had arrived and so I ought to eat. They had grown the vegetables themselves and I should try them.

She said that on this, my fist visit to the cave, there was no dripping water. Several years ago the master on the great platform, having heard that this cave was a desirable piece of real estate, and that the Zen master on Mount Kuifengshan had once lived here, rushed over to have a look. The result was that the cave which had originally been as dry as a bone, started to drip with water from no one knows where as soon as he arrived. If the roof of the cave dripped water it was uninhabitable. He took one look and left. The moment he left it got better. He had wanted to exchange his platform for their cave.

She said living here is a matter of destiny. Before they came here they lived on the hat shaped peak above the Caotang Temple where an old master was the abbot. They were there for many years, it was very peaceful.

The previous master who lived here couldn't stand it. She said it was too damp, she suffered from serious eczema and wanted to exchange with them, so they came. They saw that it was not a bad place and didn't feel that it was damp, it was good to live in. They brought nothing with them when they first arrived and didn't want to go down the mountain. Living in the hills you must reduce your contact with the outside world as much as possible and live on a few herbs. Although time and again you may reject contact with the outside world, there will always be people who will come looking for you. There is a lay person from the south who often comes up bringing the necessities of life for them.

Why must practitioners reduce contact with the outside world? For worldly people it is either love or hate. We leave our homes to take up Buddhism in order to separate ourselves from the mundane world of dust. Of course, at some point in the future they will want to go off the mountain but that point has not yet arrived. Generally, they lived in a place in three year stretches, they were into their second three year period here. They were quite attached to this place for the first three years but now if needs, they could leave this meal uneaten, shoulder their knapsacks and be off.

The little master brought the *jiaozi*, lit incense in front of the statue of the Buddha, recited an incantation and presented the food. The *jiaozi* were succulent and seeing that I was young they filled the dish so that I eat until I wanted to give up food altogether before I was allowed to put down my chopsticks. Despite the fact that this was just a simple vegetarian meal of *jiaozi*, it remains the deepest impression of my time in the mountains.

The elderly nun had become a buddhist at the Buddhist College at Mount Wutaishan. She had been in ill health at senior high school and had gone to the college and later become a buddhist. She told me that her disciple had become a buddhist twice, the first time, her family had got her back but she had later secretly made her way to the Southern Hills alone. They had met in the Southern Hills and had practiced together. They had now been together for nine years.

As I was about to leave, this practitioner warned me to keep a pure mind always, and to guard and protect the purest seeds of my heart from pollution, they would have a natural role later; I should always see the perfection in other people, everybody was a buddha.

There was a secret cave at the bottom of the mountain. I had heard Master Yijing say that very few people visited it, it was called Dayudong Cave. The master who lived there got down the mountain just once or twice in a year. It was surrounded by grass and had no contact with the outside world. When I asked the old nun for directions, she burst into laughter and said that the place was like the magic rock that gave birth to the Monkey King[1] and the master there lived in its stomach. When you're in the valley use the rock above this cave as a marker and you'll find it. The door to the cave closed behind me but I could still hear the old nun's delighted laughter.

Descending the gorge from the Guanyin cave, a simple path

---

1 Sun Wukong, a monkey with miraculous powers who figures in the classical novel *Journey to the West*. ——*Trans*

had been trodden through the grass. At the height of summer, like a swimmer. you had to part the grass that submerged everything before you could move. At the center of the valley I found spring water pouring down the precipice and in the water a water pipe that carried it on down. There was also a vegetable patch and I thought that I should soon arrive at the Dayudong Cave that I was looking for. But could there be a great rock in a place like this? On the way, I had imagined what the Dayudong Cave would be like: an enormous rock on top of a precipice, a cave in it, and a monk seated outside meditating.

The Dayudong Cave appeared close to the precipice, a huge rock with the size of three rooms. In the rock there was a cave that faced south and in front of the entrance to the cave was a straw hut with tomatoes growing in its courtyard. Master Yangqing was sitting meditating in front of a stone table at the entrance to the cave. He seemed to know that I was coming and had already set out the utensils for tea drinking.

Master Yangqing had become a buddhist several decades ago and had lived on Mount Yunju and at the Wolong Temple below. He said that he had lived in almost all the Zen halls in the country, he had just come back from a spell at the Shaolin Temple. He had studied *Qigong* when young and had been close to the famous masters of *Qigong* such as Zhang Yansheng and Pang Heming. He had also taught *Qigong* at the country's largest *Qigong* academy.

He told me that he had a fellow master of considerable skill and who was able to comprehend without thinking. For example when steaming *mantou*[1] he never looked at the time and naturally knew when they were done. This ability is the instant comprehension of the consciousness-only school of

---

1 A kind of steamed bun made from wheat flour. —*Trans*

Buddhism. It is the same as when just after going to sleep, you open your eyes and see every form and object and know of their existence and their names without thinking about it or distinguishing one from the other.

Why is it that nowadays there are relatively few practitioners of any attainment? It is because our minds are unfocussed, and that from childhood onwards there has been too much distraction, these bad habits are difficult to eradicate. Practice is like exerting one's energy. If the energy is not concentrated there is insufficient strength. People's abilities differ, take the ancients shooting the drum for example, normally people could only shoot through one drum skin, but those with the ability could penetrate seven skins with one arrow.

Master Yangqing was quite thin and tall with long ears. His manner put me in mind of a buddha in a certain wall-painting. He spoke slowly and listening to him was soporific.

At dusk, the sun shone on the mountain opposite so that it sparkled with gold, hawks circled above the precipice and the colors in the valley darkened to a pitch black. Master Yangqing wanted to cook noodles and keep me to eat with him. I hurriedly said goodbye, intending to go over the mountain ridge and seek lodging for the night at the Lion Hut on the other side.

When I left Master Yangqing wanted me to take some tomatoes that he had grown and also to give some to Zen Master Benxu at the Lion Hut. As night fell I finally saw the Lion Hut where Elder Monk Xuyun had once practiced. At the time, he had first built a hut further down at Shizi (Lion) Rock but it was too far to go down the mountain to fetch water and he just used melted snow and rain water. His staple diet was potatoes, every year he planted 365 clamps of potatoes and eat a clamp a day, as many as there were to a clamp, as fate willed it. His bed was only three foot long, hardly enough to sleep in.

He looked at the clouds drifting to and fro over the mountain ridge opposite but the emptiness remained unmoved, hence his title Xuyun (Empty Cloud).

In the final month of one particular year, Elder Monk Xuyun washed some potatoes, put them in a pot to boil and then begun to meditate, intending to eat the potatoes when they had cooked. Outside, the hills were covered in snow and the wind cut to the bone but with tranquil body and mind he gradually entered a state of Zen calm. On the sixth day of the first month of the next year, the three masters Jiechen, Yuexia and Fucheng from a nearby hut came to wish him a happy New Year. When they reached the entrance they found the snow in front of the door covered in tiger's footprints and concluded that the tiger must have eaten him. Inside they found the old monk still deep in meditation. They called to him several times without response and eventually knocked on the chimes to wake him from meditation. When he was awake they asked him whether he had eaten. He replied that the potatoes should be done by now. They looked into the pot to find that the potatoes were covered in mould—over 20 days had passed.

Beneath the Elder Monk Xuyun's stupa there were two huts, one was occupied by Zen Master Benxu and the other was that of his disciple Master Shengde.

I was just in time for supper with a lavish selection of vegetables, rice, roasted potatoes and fresh cucumber. The master had grown all the vegetables himself.

Zen Master Benxu was thin and vigorous looking with clear eyes. He disliked talking and spent the greater part of his time reading or meditating. I had heard a practitioner say that Master Benxu had once been sitting in meditation in the dilapidated hut that had previously existed on this spot when a

▶ Zen master Benxu of the Lion Hut (Photo/Zhang Jianfeng)

huge rock had rolled down the mountain and crushed the rear wall, stopping inches from him. Early next day he had moved out of the hut that had been destroyed and built the Lion Hut anew.

A light rain began to fall after supper and Master Benxu took me to visit Elder Monk Xuyun's stupa. The relics came from Yunjushan and Master Benxu had mobilized lay people and monks to subscribe to the erection of this stupa which would stand for ever amidst the trees on this mountain. In the future many more people would come and visit.

Lion Mountain was the peak of the mountains behind Jiawutai and was shaped like a reclining male lion. Behind the hut was Lion Rock, about ten feet high. Elder Monk Xuyun's Lion Hut had originally been built against Lion Rock but by the time that Master Benxu arrived, it had been abandoned and he had built the present hut on its site.

Behind the hut Master Benxu pointed out to me traces of the hut that the old monk had built here on Lion Rock and a stone wall that had been blackened by smoke from a fire.

The old monk had lived here half a century ago, the clouds were always changing, everything had changed and only the rock was the same as before. But the clouds were old friends and were now Zen Master Benxu's neighbors.

One day in the rainy season I visited the Lion Hut once more. I had been too simple in my visualization of the route through the gorge and it was already dark by the time that I scrambled up to the Lion Hut in the rain. My shoes had been soaked through by the rain and when I saw Master Benxu I emitted a long gasp, he was just listening to the live broadcast of the ascent of the Chinese spacecraft Shenzhou–7. I sat beside the stove drying my shoes and trousers, his disciple cooked me a washing bowl full of instant noodles and I eat the lot.

This time I could sit and talk with him in a relaxed manner.

A lama had been living here when he first arrived 13 years ago, he had left the hut to Zen Master Benxu and had wandered away. At that time, the hut was as it was when Master Xuyun had lived in it and in the ensuing half century the hut had almost never lacked the presence of a practitioner. The surrounding wall was the original, but the roof was now tiled rather than thatched. Previously, the hut had let in the wind through all four walls and the third winter after Master Benxu's arrival, the snow had been waist deep. One day a party of people had suddenly appeared, climbing up through the gorge, amongst them was an old man who burst into tears on seeing him. The old man said that he suffered from an incurable disease and that the day he was to die had already been foretold. However, it had all been changed by a dream.

In the dream, a monk had cured him by rubbing the crown of his head. Full of gratitude, he had asked the monk where he lived. The monk had said that he lived at the Lion Hut in the Southern Hills. Several days later he was restored to health. He had enquired widely of the Lion Hut and had subsequently heard that there was indeed a Lion Hut in the Southern Hills. Today, he had found it at last. The old man said that the monk in the dream had been Zen Master Benxu.

The old man burst into tears again when he had seen the hardship of life here. He had later organized everybody into repairing the hut and putting monk Xuyun's stupa in good repair.

It was 2,000 meters above sea-level. Down on the plain, a month would have been long enough to build a stupa. But here the bricks had to be carried up six hours from the point beyond which vehicles were unable to proceed and from winter to winter it took three years to complete the stupa. The bricks were carried up through the snow and during the course of the journey, a fire had had to be lit three times against the

▲ Master Benxu in seated Zen meditation in the snow (Photo/Master Benxu's disciple Shi Shengde)

cold. A number of hill dwellers had lost teeth through falling when carrying up sand. There was a little girl of just twelve who carried 40 kilos of bricks on her back and was scolded by her father if she faltered on the way. Hill dwellers lead an impoverished life. Off the mountain, people would be unlikely to do this kind of work even if you paid them.

Below Xuyun's stupa there was a small retreat house where there had been no break in the succession of practitioners going into retreat. Each time there was somebody in retreat they had undertaken to look after them and had taken them food. Zen Master Benxu said that this place was very conducive to achievement, people who had been in retreat here had all said that they felt very tranquil sitting there.

A family of cat practitioners now lived in the retreat hut. When I went in, two large cats twisted out from beneath the quilt on the *kang* and looked me over curiously with an aloof air. They had a litter of ten kittens. There had been nobody in retreat during the last six months and this had become their domain, Zen Master Benxu looked after them personally and brought food for the whole family at noon.

Occasionally they went and stayed at the Dayudong Cave as guests of Master Yangqing. He had just harvested his walnuts when they went. He said that, fortunately, he had been quicker than the squirrels, he had knocked the walnuts down leaving not one on the tree, the squirrels had leaped up the tree to get them, had looked left and right and couldn't believe their eyes. Zen Master Benxu said that his disciple had gathered practitioners from other species in the mountains who came seeking alms in the winter. They were pica birds, pigeons and eagles.

The squirrel practitioners' buddhist name was Anxin, they were a pack and often came to eat after snow had fallen. They sat outside the window early in the morning and tapped on the glass, they also queued up to eat. The eagle never harmed the smaller animals here even in the winter.

A yellow fox was often a guest in the courtyard and sometimes fought with the civet while they looked on as spectators.

I once saw a short film about practitioners in the Southern Hills in which, over ten years ago a group of people from the south had come to the Southern Hills. When they called on Zen Master Benxu, they had found that he was in the sixth day of a nearly completed seven day fast. The group had wanted to enquire about the situation in the hills. When they invited him out of the hut, he had already completed one seven day fast. A seven day fast means taking no food at all for seven days, just water. Zen Master Benxu said that of course nobody would starve to death as the result of fasting for seven days, eating was just a habit. In fact, as long as you were pure in thought very little food was required for the maintenance of life. If, on the third day of a fast the desire to eat was too strong, it could be suppressed. Beyond three days there was no desire for food and the mind was much more alert. There were no distracting thoughts, mental chaos never arose and, moreover, the bodily senses became more relaxed.

Despite fasting, the lavatory still had to be used, though what was passed was garbage that had been in the body for years, undigestible food eaten as a child for example. The body was beyond comprehension.

Master Benxu said that a daoist priest who lived in Foyezhang only ate two ounces of the herb Solomon's seal a day and had not eaten cereals or grain for over ten years. For years he had sat without sleeping and had never lain down.

There was a practice of seated Zen called inner contemplation. For much of the time our mind was like a cloud of dust, never still, swirling about in the wake of things outside the body and thus giving rise to chaotic thought. Because of the mind's failure to overcome the material world, it was mired in likes and dislikes, lost in love and desire, anger and hate, it had lost sight of its original true form. Sometimes the self did not know what it was doing. It was the present, the instant, that was all important. It was impossible to live in the past, it had already disappeared without trace; nor in the future, since it would always be impossible to control.

Inner contemplation was a relaxation of mind and body, a clearing of the mind of everything, attending to one's internal body, concentrating thought upon the five internal organs, like so many suspended chime bells in their brilliance, so that in the end one could understand each and every vein and artery of one's body, much as if you were looking at somebody else. Zen Master Benxu had come to understand his own body through this form of seated Zen. Once, in practice, he had suddenly seen himself as if he were looking at somebody else, a state of amazement in which nothing else existed. Master Benxu said that this phenomenon was an outflow of spiritual knowledge. When someone was relaxed and their innermost being was in a state of exceptional tranquility, the consciousness could flow like water. At that point you felt that the self was unlimited in size and that you could even sense the wind on the distant grass. In the beginning he had mainly practiced Zen, though later he had recited the names of the Buddha as well. He could now subdue vexations, not one could arise, there was no antipathy or hatred for anyone.

Over ten years ago, a novice monk had heard that there was a hut in this gorge and wished to come and live here. At the time there was no clear path up the gorge and he became lost and spent a night on the mountainside. Early next morning he heard the sound of the wooden fish clapper, now near, now far, drawing him towards the Lion Hut—at the time none of the practitioners living in the gorge had a wooden fish clapper.

On one occasion, several practitioners had arrived at the Lion Hut. Generally, practitioners visited the hall for prayer in the morning but at three o'clock in the morning he had heard somebody in the hall, the chimes had sounded and someone was chanting. He got up and found that everybody was asleep and that the sound was coming from the surroundings of the hut.

He had often heard of people saying that they had met a hermit priest in the hills, who, by his appearance seemed to be about thirty years old. When asked how long he had lived in the hills he replied that it had been for more than thirty years. The Southern Hills were more than 400 *li* across and there were people living in seclusion in every valley. There were still gorges and peaks out of reach of the ordinary mortal where practitioners lived in seclusion.

Several years earlier a lay person had sought out Master Benxu to take the tonsure from him and become a buddhist. Master Benxu said that becoming a buddhist was a matter of affinity and suggested that he should stay at the hut for a few days to see if he was suitable. One day the practitioner dreamed that he saw Old Monk Xuyun writing the characters for "Practice the Mind through Experience of the World" for him. Master Benxu said that it was Xuyun revealing that he should return to the world to practice. The practitioner then went back down the mountain.

Thirteen years previously, Master Benxu had had three disciples who were now wandering abroad but who would eventually return here.

That night I slept in the retreat hut, through the wall behind the bed were the ruins of the hut where the monk Xuyun had entered the state of Zen calm. I dreamed strangely that Master Benxu had changed into Monk Xuyun and was meditating in the sitting position with three other elder monks.

In the 50 years since the departure of Monk Xuyun, many practitioners had passed through here and Zen Master Benxu had lived here the longest. He said that perhaps he should be leaving soon as well, it was all a matter of destiny.

Mother Miaolian's Tianbao Maopeng (Hut of the Heavenly Jewel) lay deep in the valley in thick forest and I saw, written in the eaves, the words "Cease speech".

She had lived here for many years. There were two rooms that seemed to have some history. The eating area was damp and all the walls were built of stone.

The room in which I was to spend the night contained a large *kang* and because the roof leaked badly, there was damp where the *kang* was. The leak had been stuffed with an old sheet which reduced the leaking rain water a little. The sound of the wooden fish reached my ears through the falling rain and I fell asleep to its sound.

When I pushed open the door early next morning, the rain hung from the eaves in threads of translucent crystal. The mountain valley was a formless mass and, within the fog nothing existed, it seemed a void in which everything of yesterday had been transformed.

Breakfast was freshly steamed *mantou* and I eat the vegetables grown by Mother Miaolian, rather extravagantly cooked in oil, which made me a little uncomfortable.

After the rain stopped, I prepared to go down the mountain. Mother Miaolian hurriedly emerged from her room running her buddhist beads through her fingers and gesturing to me to stop. Seeing that I was determined to go on down she produced an umbrella that she insisted I should take. I refused but the umbrella was thrust into my hand nevertheless.

I left reluctantly and in the distance, Mother Miaolian stood in the drizzle at the highest point of the courtyard with her arms crossed in buddhist salutation.

Over a month later, I stood once more in the courtyard of the Tianbao Maopeng and Mother Miaolian had completed her vow of silence. She told me that when she had first arrived there was nowhere to live and she had found a cave further down, filled with deer or goat's dung. She had been grateful to be able to sleep there and had felt that it was a paradise of tranquility. She had later discovered this abandoned hut, repaired it and then moved in. There had been no water when she arrived and she had had to go downstream in the valley and carry it back on a shoulder pole. In the winter she had melted snow for drinking water. Later on water had become more and more plentiful and never ran out. She had built a channel

to lead it in to the river valley and another to the courtyard so that the murmuring water flowed through it.

Mother Miaolian said that as long as you let go of everything, the leaves on the trees on the mountainside would be enough to eat and would last a lifetime. When you really let go of everything you would never run out of food or run out of water.

Daoists never die of starvation.

Before she had come to the Southern Hills she had built a number of large temples in Hebei province. Once built she had invited other practitioners to move in and live there while she herself had moved here. Practitioners from distant Hebei often came to seek her out and support her, they cooked for her and looked after her. In the future, she intended to build a hall of worship alongside the hut for the convenience of the practitioners of the future.

I had heard Master Benxu of the Lion Hut above say that he had often heard the sound of a wooden fish clapper in the valley, sometimes close by, sometimes in the distance. Mother Miaolian said that she, too, often heard things, sometimes the sound of the wooden fish and sometimes the sound of the instruments of worship. The sound came from beside the hut where she lived. It was often at about three o'clock in the morning, she took it as the sound of the chimes and rose to perform the morning service. There was nobody else in the valley, the sound was beyond comprehension.

Sometimes she could hear people calling to her as she was sitting in meditation at night. Sometimes it was a male voice, sometimes a female. None of this was to be taken notice of, whole hearted practice was all that mattered. She could sit in meditation reciting the sutras for a day and a night, often

◀ A practitioner chopping firewood (Photo/Zhang Jianfeng)

sleeping an hour during the evening and then reciting into the following day.

Mother Miaolian said, look at the water, it does not stop for an instant, the ancient masters could achieve enlightenment by watching the water, it is all impermanence, the unstopping instant. A blade of grass, the four seasons, the changes from withering to blossom are examples of impermanence as well.

You will have nothing that you cannot let go as you observe all this. If there are still things hooked into your mind, there is no point in speaking of practice.

We stood by the stream in the courtyard, its water so clear that you could see your expression in it. Two thousand years ago the fishermen sang:

> Blue water so clear, I could wash the red tassels on my hat
> Blue water so muddy, I could wash my feet.

The water could wash my mind clean of all the dust of the world.

The mist rose from the valley and the rain of the Southern Hills seemed to turn green. As I drifted amongst the misty peaks of these blue hills clad in a raincoat of rushes, I had long ago forgotten the time of return.

Chapter Five

The Dayi Valley
—Home To Those Who Roam

Amidst the vastness of the Southern Hills, it is beside the Dayu River that hermits are to be found in their numbers. I passed the Leigushi village and followed the great autumn river upstream. Although it was pouring with rain the river water was dark green and brought to mind the words of a hermit who lived on the banks of the Feng River:

Green water flows from the mountain gate,
Headlong towards the reddened dust.
On this path to the worldly way
Can it keep its purity?

He is writing of the grief of the green water flowing from the river valley in its unblemished purity on its way to meet a polluted fate.

By the side of the river I met a scholarly-looking and emaciated young practitioner wearing very strong glasses. His hair and beard were long and his blue turned grey shirt looked as if it had not been washed for years. With his straw sandals, staff and heavy pack, I thought he must be a buddhist *shami* not long into his novitiate.

He told me that a hermit had entrusted him with the task of delivering supplies to a Zen master who lived in a cave beneath Mount Rentoushan. I looked back and saw that his companion too wore strong glasses. Although they had long departed the red dust of the world the experience of study had obviously left them with a souvenir for life.

They lived in the Wenshu Cave above the Leigushi village. Having said goodbye to them I decided to take a look there in the future.

The mountain rain crouched within the clouds as they floated at will, delivering a shower here or there and when unoccupied, flying over the sacred hills as care-free and uninhibited as the poet Li Bai (701 – 762, one of most prominent poets in China).

I had forgotten the umbrella when I left the Lion Hut and after several hours walking in the rain I longed for the warmth of a fire.

As dusk approached I asked the way from a hill dweller and following his directions climbed up through a steep valley. The valley was piled high with boulders, trees scattered amongst the larger boulders and mud huts scattered amongst the trees. There were few hill dwellers in the valley, it was mostly the huts of practitioners.

A mountain stream flowed through the center of the valley and snow white reeds covered the ground. I felt very old as I stood there in the dusk. I met a hill dweller behind a pile of damp firewood and he told me that the valley was home to practitioners, there were four or five daoists, a daoist nun, five or six buddhist monks and a lay buddhist.

I saw a hut above his courtyard where the practitioner was cooking supper. I set down my pack and sat and attended to the fire—solving the problem of supper at the same time.

He said that he was disinclined to cook having eaten elsewhere in the middle of the day. Having carried in the water to wash the vegetables I sat down to the noodles. The wood had been damp and I had swallowed a great deal of saliva while waiting for this bowl of noodles.

It seemed that this monk belonged to the large-minded and contented variety of person, he spoke very slowly and listening to him was like digging a well with your bare hands, it required endless patience.

His hut was quite extensive and was divided into three rooms by mud brick walls. He said that you could say that the hut was, but you could also say that it wasn't. He had lived there for three years and before that for many years at Mount Taibai where he had been born. When he had first arrived he had lodged in a hill dwellers house. Later the owner of this house had allowed buddhists to live there and so he had cleared it up a bit. Later still, the landlord's younger brother had wanted to sell it to get a wife with the money and had reminded him several times. He could be leaving at any moment.

The hill dwellers' houses in the valley had almost all been sold. Some practitioners had been fortunate, people had raised money for them and bought them, giving the practitioners a fixed dwelling where they could apply their minds to the practice of the way. Even if they no longer lived there in the future they could let later practitioners live there.

He said that you would now need several thousand yuan to buy a hut, where could buddhists who lived deep in the hills find such a sum? Wasn't it now the same as for people in the towns? Moreover, not every practitioner would be able to find one of those caves.

After supper, I washed my feet and got on to the *kang*. In the night, there was just the sound of the wind in the roof, while not too far away the river water raced on with a sound like the roaring of wild beasts. We sat crossed legged by the light of a candle and talked through the night.

The monk produced his notebook, filled with forms

of address: Father, Son, Son-in-Law, Grandson, Paternal Grandfather, Elder Brother, Younger Brother, Older Male Cousin, Younger Male Cousin, Uncle, Nephew, Maternal Uncle, Sister's Son, Master, Disciple, Leader, Subordinate … all these, he said, were you.

A person might be very simple but he might also be required to play numberless roles in the world. As in acting, there were very many people who were too immersed in the theater of life, once in character it was impossible to free oneself.

Many people knew that life was a process of addition and subtraction. As you grew up you were adding all the time, diploma, work, money, house, car, marriage, children, grandchildren but then came subtraction. In truth we were like a foolish child who once having grabbed something would not let it go. We piled so much on our minds that we only reluctantly gave up as we drew the last breath of our lives. There were many people who could take up but not let go, the first thing that buddhists had to do was to let go utterly.

This hut occupied the space between is and is not as did everything in the world. There is a saying, take off your shoes and socks today not knowing whether you will wear them tomorrow. What is the point of so much anxiety?

In the end, the question that faced all those who lived in the hills was the "return to truth". The return to truth was about the destination of your spirit.

He had met some of those who had lived and managed well in the hills and had achieved much. Later they left the mountain to set up temples below. At that point, discord had appeared with vexation in its wake. Actions gave rise to ideas, ideas required an investment, once you did something that other people could see, it was no longer something that you alone could control, this was when discord arose. It was after having gained something that you never knew where to place your heart. There were many examples of this.

He had no interest in creating a Bodhimanda or place of enlightenment. What he wished to do was to go on waiting. This was no easy matter.

If one practiced with diligence it was easy to get going, without it you would remain at the starting point for the whole of your life.

Sleep started from I know not where and I woke in the latter half of the night to realize that I had slept a long time and that the monk had gone to sleep sitting in the meditating position. The noise of water outside sounded in the air for an instant and then faded, though as I listened it seemed never to stop.

The golden light of early morning shone through the wooden shutters, so strong that it was impossible to open the eyes, a new day had started and birdsong endlessly enlarged the space of the valley. I went to the riverside to wash my face with water and carried back two bucketfuls on a shoulder pole. The monk was already cooking a gruel of millet and when I had finished eating I went to call on some daoist masters who lived further up the valley.

A mountain path set about with swaying chrysanthemums led me to the front of a hut that had no surrounding wall where two daoists were drying pine nuts under the persimmon trees in the courtyard.

They were both disciples of Master Tan who was down the mountain visiting Baxian An Temple (the Temple of the Eight Immortals), he had lived here for over ten years.

I sat in the courtyard in the sun chatting with these two young daoists.

Master Wang came from Mount Laoshan in Shandong province and had recently arrived here from the depths of

Mount Taibai. He said that there were still quite a number of daoists there, but they were mostly quite elderly. He hadn't had time to dig up the potatoes that he had planted and had left them to somebody else.

In the upper part of the valley he had found a large boulder with a cave the size of two rooms underneath. Alongside there was a spring which flowed from beneath two large rocks. I saw that he was in the process of altering this cave dwelling and had built a small window that faced the sun. The cave was damp and water seeped from between the rocks. Master Tan had supervised the digging of two deep drains in the floor of the cave to form an underground channel. He planned to cover them with stones which would make the place much better to live in. It would make an ideal dwelling once it had been altered. Until the alterations had been completed he was staying temporarily with Master Tan.

In Master Wang's room I saw an end blown flute (*dongxiao*) hanging on the book case. He often went up the mountain opposite to play it, he had a partner there—an arctic fox. It was said that arctic foxes practiced for a thousand years and could take human shape. The fox frequently kept him company, it had no fear of man. He often spoke with it, it came and went invisibly, there was no particular time and it would often appear suddenly.

I teasingly suggested to Master Wang that he could make the arctic fox into his fairy companion. He gave an embarrassed laugh and said, who was there who would not want to have a fairy companion with whom he could practice?

Master Wang had the temperament of a classical scholar, calm and gracious. He invited me to eat some of the pine nuts that he had prepared for winter, they were much better than those on sale off the mountain. It was the first time that I had eaten them raw and my mouth was full of saliva. Master Wang said that I had an affinity with the way, hill dwellers dare not eat freshly picked pine nuts, they were too bitter.

Master Wang did not like talking and was only interested in silence, half a day could pass without a word from him. He was always working: stocking up with food for the winter, a pile of pine nuts drying in the sun, a pile of pine cones just picked from the tree.

The poet Tao Yuanming had his stringless *qin* and often sat beside a stream strumming soundlessly, only a soul-mate could comprehend it. Master Tan's other pupil, Master Huang, had an ancient zither (*guzheng*).

There was a cave at the top of the mountain's blue peak where the footprints of deer and fox were often to be found, a place forgotten by man. This was where Master Huang lived. In the early morning the sun rose on the opposite side and turned the rocks and crags to gold; at night moonlight seemed to clothe the mountain top in a layer of fine white paper. He often sat with his zither on a rock beside the stream and plucked the strings for the moon to hear. He had selected his daoist name "Ruoshui" (Resembling Water) from the works of Laozi, the founder of Daoism.

Master Huang was well built, his family came from the distant northeast. He said that he had left home to be a daoist because thought and habit had very naturally set him upon this road. Just at the time when his secular life was at its richest he had let go of everything, he had given up everything in its entirety.

Before leaving home to become a daoist he had not lacked for money, he was the youngest in the family, much was taken care of for him and he could rely on others. He said that he had not achieved enlightenment in the last few decades, not until sickness had sought him out. Just when he was intent upon amusement, fine living and all the worldly pleasures, he had

been afflicted by illness.

In 2006 he had spent two weeks alone in a room by himself. He did not eat or drink a mouthful for three days. People said that you would die if you did not eat for seven days. Afterwards he had eaten some fruit but by the time he had reached the seventh day he was afraid and had recorded all his thoughts for his family. His elder sister, wife and children had given too much to him and there was no way that he could repay them. Later, as his mind gradually began to let go of things, he felt well, mentally alert and clear-headed. Many illnesses are acquired through eating, people have to gorge themselves before they can be satisfied. There were many things that the ancients did not eat but nowadays we had no inhibitions and discussed what on the earth and in the seas we had not eaten.

He had originally intended to carry on for a month, the sensation had been unimaginable. He had thought of much during that period and had considered all the 30 years and more of his life. He had felt that his whole being was being transformed.

Had it been his former self, he would have felt his subsequent actions to be very strange. When he had been studying engraving in Fujian province he had worn a pair of old Beijing cloth shoes and if someone had admired them he had then bought ten pairs and given them to him as a gift.

When he had done this he had asked himself if he could really let go.

At the time he had no thought of leaving home and the secular life.

He had been fond of travel from childhood and had often gone travelling with a pack on his back. On a trip to Dali in Yunnan province, he had met his master in the street. His

◀ A rear view of daoist master Huang (Photo/Zhang Jianfeng)

143

master had been carrying a pack on which was written: "For you, a cure for all ills." This had aroused his curiosity because much of what had happened to him had been caused by illness. He thought of the fact that his illness had remained uncured for over 20 years and wondered what profound medical skills this daoist might have.

The master was buying silver ornaments on the streets of Dali and fearful of being duped he had followed him wherever he went. He had not wanted to accost the master and then in a moment of negligent concentration the master had disappeared from sight. In a street that was 50 to 60 meters in length not a person was to be seen. He was even more curious, put down his things and raced forward in pursuit and found the master making a call from a telephone booth. The master was about 70 years of age at the time.

Afterwards, the two strangers had spent seven or eight days together and although it was rather a mystery to be with the master, the emotional ties had been stronger than that between father and son. Later, the master had taken him as a pupil and had instructed him to leave home and go to the Laojun Cave in Chongqing to practice. He had visited many places together with his master who cured sickness without charge. He established a relationship with his patients who gave him 50 cents or one yuan. When they returned and counted the money, to their surprise there was often 50 to 60 yuan. It was odd that practitioners did not seek money but somehow obtained it.

The master roamed, from Xinjiang to Tibet and from Tibet to Yunnan, roaming ceaselessly from place to place without stopping. Despite his age and the several tens of kilos weight of his pack he still walked like the wind.

The master had told him that he would first have to learn how to conduct himself before he could teach him anything.

A very long time ago, a master would have taught a pupil preparing to follow the way some of the techniques employed to promote it. However, some people had used these techniques, arts and skills for nefarious purposes. Subsequently masters had taught those seeking the way how to be in accord with virtue before talking of other things.

Master Huang said, you know, the way is not something that can be comprehended in a day, it is hidden, buried like gold. The sun is always in the sky and is sometimes obscured by black clouds, but it is still there.

In times of peace and prosperity everybody thrusts morality aside, but, in fact, it is our best remedy. By the time we realize that it is time to take medicine, the illness is already serious. If we ignore the way (morality) the crisis is upon us, we do not sense it. We are like fish caught unaware in a net, when they do realize, it is already far too late.

It is only in the face of disaster that people come to their senses, but over a long period they can become confused. We never know why disaster may overtake us. In fact, it is not a matter of chance, it is just that we cannot see it, there are only a few wise men who can see all this clearly. People today do not even know themselves, let alone heaven and earth, we long ago abandoned the wisdom of the ancients.

Consequently there are some people, who, in the role of practitioner, stand on the borders of humanity and observe. They can see the problems and dangers of the majority relatively clearly. Observing those few next to you enables you to understand even more people and observing even more people enables you to understand the world as a whole.

Our mind is like a feudal king, man grows day by day from birth and slowly the robbers arrive. The more you see the more you want and at that point you lose control of your eyes, hands, and feet. Desire takes the throne, the vassal lords no longer obey and this nation of yours has been occupied by robbers. When robbers are in control lost territory must be recovered and the mind returned to its original state of purity. This is the principle that underlies the cultivation of the truth and the comprehension of the way. Children have a purity that enables them to perceive all forms of life, with and without color, with and without form. Slowly they grow, acquiring thought and speech and the ability to think, but with falsity spirituality is lost.

The cultivation of the truth is not the cultivation of anything else. Whatever you do, when you are unoccupied you must allow your mind to rest, whether it be for five minutes or for ten. The moment you sit down and let everything go, you will gradually acquire wisdom. Most people do not allow their minds a rest until the day they die and thus struggle to control the perturbations of their mind. The *Great Learning* (*Daxue*) says: "Know how to cease and then settle, settle and then achieve calm, once calm then achieve peace." It comes gradually step by step, the practice of Daoism means that you must let go of everything. If your mind is always fixed on money or anxious about wife and children the practice of Daoism will never become a reality. You will only come to know the way by putting it first.

The cultivation of the truth and the comprehension of the way is not a gift that can be bestowed upon someone. Were it so, the people could bestow it upon the nation and a father could pass it to his son, these are selfish desires. Precisely because it cannot be bestowed, so it cannot be imparted through speech. To achieve the way one must put aside personal considerations for the common good. With the least personal interest there is no way to speak of, what is said is mere theory. For example,

▶ Master Huang and his daoist friend (Photo/Zhang Jianfeng)

here there is a flight of steps, but flight of steps is just a name, it is only when you actually walk up the steps that you can know what they are.

The wise seek deficiency because consummation leads to the chance of injury. So they never reach that ultimate. Take the moon for example, it waxes from the first to the fifteenth of each lunar month and wanes from the sixteenth on, everything is life and death, rise and fall, where yin and yang (dark and light, negative and positive, female and male) are in balance. It is only at the appropriate point that there can be a guarantee of neither gain nor loss.

Master Huang said that he should know that in the practice of Daoism he would have to undergo much hardship. The way was of nature, there was much that was obtained naturally. Looking back on the path he had travelled was like Old Zhang Guo, one of the Eight Immortals, riding back to front on a donkey, in fact, he was not riding back to front, he was telling people that when they had the time, they should look back and think of how they had travelled the road and not of the delights of the past.

He said that he had not read too many books. All this existed naturally and emerged naturally when he spoke. It was certainly not something he had learned.

Having dried the pine nuts we set about lighting the fire and cooking. I had been hungry for some time and Master Huang produced the chrysanthemum *mantou* that he had steamed, remarking that they were probably the only specialty of his hut. He took some yellow daisies that he had picked and kneaded them into the *mantou* flour to steam into buns. When eaten the *mantou* had a slightly sweetish taste. The stream was behind the hut, I chopped firewood and Master Huang made the fire, the midday smoke refused to leave the room and enveloped Master Huang, leaving just a shadow, as if it had dressed him in a light blue daoist gown.

In a while, Benefactor Di, a nearby hill dweller arrived. He was a neighbor of Master Tan's whose elder brother had become a monk many years previously and naturally enjoyed the company of practitioners. He had been in the army when young and now worked as a security guard off mountain. He believed that outside visitors like me should taste their steamed potato cakes. Under his encouragement Master Wang steamed a potful of small potatoes and then pounded them into a paste in the mortar in the courtyard, added flour and kneaded it into flatbread which was then cut into squares, steamed and sprinkled with herbs.

We put up a small table by the stream next to the courtyard with a bowlful of potato cakes each. When I had finished I felt as if I were drunk and very much wanted to go to sleep in the autumn sunshine.

Benefactor Di said that the Lotus Cave was not far away and he would be willing to take me to see it. It was the place where the famous elder monk Yinguang (1862 – 1940) of the Republic had become a monk. Neither Master Wang nor Master Huang had been there and we decided to walk over the hills and visit it together early next morning.

Early next morning, by the time that I woke to the sound of birdsong, the others had already prepared the *mantou* and pine nuts that we were to eat on the way. With our knapsacks on our backs we crossed two ranges of hills in three hours on our way to the Lotus Cave. The spring water beneath the cave was clear and cold and the cave itself was occupied by a lay buddhist and a monk who looked after the incense.

By the time that we returned from the cave Master Tan had already gone back to his hut.

When I saw Master Tan he had been digging potatoes, his hands covered in calluses. Had it not been for his topknot

of coiled hair, at first sight I would have taken him for a hill dweller. I asked him how he practiced amongst the hills, he said that he practiced nothing and just worked the land to keep himself and passed the days in following his destiny.

I asked the daoist master whether he felt tranquil in the hills. He replied that true tranquility was to be found in one's own mind. The most beautiful scenery lays within the mind and not outside. Living in the hills was not to live in the hills and just to follow destiny. If he were to describe the real reason for living in the hills it would be because it was comparatively secluded and suitable for him, nothing else.

Master Tan had worn his daoist gown for 40 years, before that it had been worn for more than 20 years by Master Huang of the Temple of the Eight Immortals. The color of its sleeves did not match and as the sleeves had shrunk over the 40 years that Master Tan had worn it band upon band of material had been added. Master Huang said that Master Tan had not bathed for over 20 years and had only ever worn this particular gown which had never been washed. Sitting beside him I only smelled the fragrance of grass and trees. I asked him whether he did not feel cold wearing such a flimsy gown.

He said, like a wild animal in the mountains, where is the cold?

Master Tan had not slept in a bed for over 30 years, he had just spread a mat on the ground. The mat was small about a square meter in size and I could not see how he slept. His quilt was never aired but was never moldy or damp.

The Chaoyang cave was at the bottom of a cliff in the upper part of the valley where the sun shone from morn till night and the thickest mists stayed away. Wild boar furrowed the earth beside Master Tan's vegetable patch every night but never

◀ Master Tan's Chaoyang Cave (Photo/Zhang Jianfeng)

touched his actual patch.

I had heard stories of Master Tan from Master Huang: In his youth, at the time of the campaign against the Four Pests (flies, mosquitoes, rats and sparrows) in 1958, Master Tan had killed 20,000 rats. He had killed a particularly large rat which had later come to haunt his dreams. Later on, he had lost his sight and the same year he had twice dreamed of two daoists who had urged him to leave home and follow the way, he had later done so and his eyesight had miraculously been restored.

Thirteen years ago, he had dreamed the same dream over and over again, in it had seen a cave, the Chaoyang cave which he had later found.

Seeing my interest in hermits and living in the mountains, Master Tan said that we could have a chat though his Hunan accent made understanding an effort. He said the way was everywhere, it was embodied in the Chinese written language. The dot and downward stroke at the top of the character *dao* (道) represents yin and yang, the horizontal stroke represents well-being, well-being gives rise to nature *zi* (自) which contains the sun *ri* (日) and moon *yue* (月) and the walking radical *zou* (辶) represents energy in motion.

Why were there so many natural disasters at present, he asked, we brought natural disasters upon ourselves. The *Responses of Taishang* (*taishang ganying pian*)[1] states: there are no entrances to fortune and disaster, man brings them upon himself. The life of the ancients contained many taboos, for example, one could not start on a long journey or work in the *xu* period (7 to 9 p.m.) *Xu* was the earth mother, every month

---

1 An early daoist work dating from at least the Song dynasty which may have been in circulation much earlier.—*Trans*

▶ Daoist master Tan hoeing his potato patch (Photo/Zhang Jianfeng)

contained a *xu* day when it was inadvisable to undertake any activity. People today, however, were utterly without taboos and had dug all the coal out of the earth. The planet was a living organism as well, its ecological balance had been damaged, how could there not be disasters?

In the practice of the way, the cultivation of the person took precedence. Humanity or the way of the person was difficult to practice and the way of the immortals difficult to achieve, to conduct oneself perfectly approached sage-hood and was not far from being immortal. A person could only acquire wisdom through purity and the absence of desires and demands. Demands led to loss of wisdom. If you sought blessings your heart and mind would be confused. If you performed good deeds you would not go unblessed. For example, someone who was selfless and acted for the common good and thought only of others would naturally receive the help of all when in difficulties, so where was the point in making demands? Most things in this world were sought but not attained.

The occupant of a hut in the depths of the valley arrived before supper. His conversation with Master Huang was full of the music of running water and being at one with plum blossom and cranes. Master Huang said that after living in the hills for many years he had come to appreciate the sound of water in the valley, understanding the tune that the water was playing was much more interesting than playing a tune oneself. I listened to the sound of running water, it was probably playing the tune *Water in the High Mountains*.

Benefactor Di and Master Wang then set about pounding potatoes and walnuts. It was difficult to get so many people together in one place in the mountains and so they were going to cook another meal of potato cakes.

It was said that Benefactor Di knew many spells, but they were not all effective. He also had some strange ideas and said that snakes were very intelligent, every autumn they came looking for the *lingzhi* fungus, without the fungus in their mouths they would not get into the mountain caves to hibernate. This was a weird idea and I had no means of checking its authenticity. He said that it was marvelous for people who watched stars. When they gazed at the stars in the heavens, it was like watching television. Based on differences in time, the stars changed position, adopting the single line snake formation, the eight trigram formation and the arhat formation from the more than 60 formations of military theory.

Benefactor Di did not want people searching him out to tell fortunes. He said that forecasting disaster or fortunes for other people disturbed the gods, communicating with spirits or heaven and earth was for helping others, not for improving one's own life. He only thought to sell his own labor for money, he had physical strength and a set of skills, and he understood herbal medicine.

Many of the huts that I had visited in the hills had their own names, but Nanshan Sanren's hut had no name. He said that you could call it what you wished.

The valley where Nanshan Sanren lived was enclosed by mountains on all sides, a small stream flowed beneath the wall of the courtyard. I stopped at a barrier of huge pine trees, the other side of the fence, there was a series of pools, large and small, each pool reflecting the sun and clouds. The path within the fence ended at a mountain gate built from grass and reeds, the courtyard wall of tamped earth was also surmounted by a thatch of reeds.

Small birds disported themselves on the thatch of the hut and the courtyard was planted with clumps of bamboo. There was no television to be watched or broadcasts to be heard here, and no electricity. Just the wind in the pines, running water, trees and plants and spiraling white clouds.

There was a young woman seated reading in the sunshine as I stepped through the fence and despite my gentle greeting I startled her. The occupant of the hut came out and with an open expression laughingly said: Is it not a joy when friends come from afar[1], let's drink tea.

There was a table surrounded by benches under the eaves.

The occupant said that the valley had been given to him by the local hill people long ago. At the moment he was organizing some lay people in the building of huts. Since tourism will be opening up the Southern Hills over the coming few years, ever more practitioners will need to find somewhere to live. When that happens, they will be able to cultivate the way, here in this valley.

Q: How will you be able to manage so much in putting up this hut?

A: Anything is manageable as long as it is not for oneself. I cannot take this place with me. It will belong to everyone in the future.

Q: Many things exist objectively, for example current scientific development. We enjoy the benefits that science brings but at the same time suffer from its threats, for example sickness, natural crises, crises in water resources, global warming, nuclear crises, emotional crises, cloning, moral crises and so on. Mankind has never faced such punishment from nature as it does today. Does this all stem from an excessive and superstitious belief in and abuse of science?

A: Scientific development is like a cart with a wheel missing, we see the danger clearly but can you stop it? It's a

---

1 A quotation from the *Analects of Confucius*—*Trans*

problem to know who can slow it down. We all know there are many benign uses of science today and while we enjoy its benefits most people would be unwilling to see it stop or return to the past. In the face of this, are we in a situation of action or inaction?

Q: Is it a case of making people understand the damage to humanity caused by the excessive development of science and bringing about a return to the traditional morality of the ancients and an enjoyment within that morality? Or is it a case of ruin within an unfettered materialism? Of course, this may be to create problems where there are none.

A: There is neither right nor wrong in scientific development, if the heart is pure then the nation is pure.

If a true practitioner does not heed the errors of the common people and is tranquil in thought there will be no evil. If you provoke society there will be contradictions forever. These are phenomena external to the mind. If the mind is pure then the external environment will be transformed. Anything we do is natural, all we need to do is to abandon the ideas of purity and impurity.

Eager questions and relaxed replies. I wanted to continue but forgot the words.

Mist amongst the trees and wind amongst the pines, silence amongst the moss, pine needles falling, clouds in the heavens and under the eaves a lay person making tea. A stream murmured at the side and even the noise of tea being swallowed echoed through the valley.

I looked through Sanren's notes, there were some jottings on it:

One day a daoist asked: What is the way? Raising his hands and turning each palm, the daoist performed a salutation.

A monk asked: What is the buddhist law? He was knocked on his head and was asked if it hurts. Answer, of course.

Being rubbed with a stretched hand, the monk seemed to be enlightened.

Someone asked: How can one see one's own nature?

I asked: What do you hear?

Answer: The sound of birds, of water and the wind.

One day a visitor from off the mountain asked: What contribution to society does a hermit like you living in the hills make?

I replied: I do not seek achievement but seek to be without error.

Someone asked: In all these years of practice what contribution have you made?

Answer: None.

Q: Why live in the hills if you make no contribution?

A: Because I eat when hungry, sleep when tired and work happily.

Someone asked: What enlightenment have you achieved?

I raised my head towards the clouds and said indifferently to myself: Whither?

Q: Are there buddhas? Are there sentient beings?

A: There are neither.

After tea, I tried some of Sanren's chrysanthemum wine. We sat in the woods, looking at the blue sky and chatting. Sanren said that when he had first arrived, there was no hut and he had lived in a tree. Later he had moved into a cave and had only subsequently achieved the destiny to build a hut.

When I planned to go down the mountain, Sanren broke off some pine needles in the wood and gave them to me as a gift from the hills. I put them in my mouth and chewed, they were sweet and cool, perhaps this was like living in the hills, you had to be there for some time before you were aware of its flavor. Sanren asked what I could hear, I said just the sound of birds, were I to listen with a deluded mind, they would be singing a song.

Have you come at leisure to write a poem? I ask.

Sanren said, aren't we all writing poems now?

The birds are writing poems, the running water plays the zither, the wind in the pines hums a tune and the clouds dream of the dance of feathered raiment[1].

I saw Nanshan Sanren again six months later. He had seemed relaxed and carefree earlier, living in a hut in the mountains with his companion, tilling the soil and studying, collecting herbs and making tea. Now, however, there were more and more visitors and it was difficult for him to cope. Many ostensibly came to drink tea in order to listen to him talk, or ask him to cheer them up. Some who took temporary accommodation in the hut then sought permanent refuge. Visitors came from different places and took up all the space in the hut. No matter how many people awaited tea, Nanshan Sanren always unhurriedly drew fresh water, lit the fire and filled bowl after bowl of tea. One day, Sanren said that he should return to the deeper depths of the mountain where there would be more joy for him. Before he did so he intended to go and see his birthplace.

His father had eventually found him after he had moved here ten years ago. Like all fathers, Nanshan Sanren's father had fervently hoped that he would marry and raise a family. Sanren's memory of his home village had gradually faded over the years since he had left his birthplace at the age of 14 to roam the world,

Nanshan Sanren's hometown was a small hill village in Hubei province where the river was full of white cranes and the land was covered in rice fields and green bamboo. The

---

1 A Tang dynasty dance performed at court—*Trans*

people, however, were more interested in fame and profit, eating and drinking. His grandfather had been a practitioner of Chinese medicine. His father had been the local vet and healer as well. His mother had been taken ill and had died when he was 14. What had brought him to despair at the time was the fact that the doctor within the family had been at a total loss. His impression was that there had been a connection between his mother's death and his father, so that he had been unwilling to stay in that frigid family any longer and one day had left without a penny. At the time, he had wanted to go walk-about, an idea that he had had before he was 14, a wish to see the mysterious world. Much later he had walked back home from Mentougou near Beijing. Later still he had left home for the south and from there he had made his way to the Southern Hills.

Sanren said that in order to practice the way, he first needed a proper visit to his family to bring all his affinities together. Perhaps this would be his last ever visit to his family, it would require careful preparation and the company of several really good friends. I was invited to go along, another was an older scholar who constantly criticized him as well as an independent artist, a neighbor of his in the hills. We planned to drive to Hubei from Xi'an in two cars. All of this was in preparation for a return to the hills.

After he had readied his hut in the Southern Hills, Nanshan Sanren came down the mountain to see me. Usually, when he came down the mountain he chose to spend the night with close friends.

An older friend urged Nanshan Sanren to have his long hair and beard cut before going home in order to avoid people staring at him and to dispel his family's anxieties about his ability to survive. When he emerged from the barber I almost thought that it was the famous Hong Kong singing star Li Ming

▲ Nanshan Sanren's thatched hut (Photo/Zhang Jianfeng)

who stood in front of me.

In the cold winds of the first month of the lunar year Sanren went to a department store, bought a padded jacket and exchanged it for the gown that he had worn before. We pooled our resources and bought several cases of Shaanxi products like wine and dates. When all was ready Sanren smiled like a child and said that this was enough to amaze the family elders, he hadn't been home for nearly ten years, it would be the first time that he had brought so many gifts with him, and these were just the things that people at home valued. On the 14th of the month, seven of us set out by car through the Southern Hills, past Zhen'an, Wudangshan, Danjiangkou and Shennongjia towards Sanren's home village near Wuhan.

Once past Danjiangkou we left the Southern Hills and the car's satnav found Sanren's birthplace—Luotian county in Huanggang district—on its map. Luotian county is at the foot of the Dabie hills. This southern county town seemed jumbled but prosperous and I saw the sort of undistinguished buildings plastered in ceramic tiles that can be seen everywhere in China. Consequently the luxuriant bamboo groves and banana trees on all sides and the gentle hills and streams made one think, all the more, of distant and ancient villages. Once through the county town of Luotian, Sanren very quickly found a minor road to his home. There was a stream beside the road but the water bubbled yellow and was filled with brightly colored floating plastic rubbish. My dream of finding white cranes on the riverbed was shattered.

Sanren telephoned his father before we arrived at the house. When we stopped at a small grey building by the side of a pond somebody set off the firecrackers that had been already prepared. I was astonished when I got out of the car, there were buildings all around in this small village and there was rubbish everywhere, there were even piles of rubbish by the pond. We sat by a brazier breathing in the sulphurous smell of the firecrackers. Sanren's father was not good at conversation, he may have been pleasantly surprised inside but I could not detect much expression on his face and he soon went off to the kitchen to cook.

Visitors crowded into the house, they all seemed to be straight-forward and unassuming country people. Once they had settled on a long bench like kindergarten children lining up for fruit, Sanren introduced us. There were several uncles, aunts and cousins who gazed curiously and cordially on this now important "personage" within the family and Sanren introduced us separately as professor, artist and editor. Since we had drivers for the cars, some could not restrain themselves from asking Sanren whether the cars were his. In order to prevent people from thinking that practitioners were no more than beggars and to make it obvious that his life was, in fact, not bad, we spoke with one voice and said that we were all members of Sanren's entourage. This caused even more people to come visiting.

Early the following morning we went with Sanren to call on other relatives. In hills criss-crossed by paths and streams, Sanren pointed out a patch of ground on a slope, some fresh green bushes had been the tea plantation that Sanren had looked after on a contract basis when he was young. His original ambition had been to be a successful business man. Not far off was the Sizu Temple in Huangmei county where he had converted to Buddhism and studied martial arts, he had also worked in the fields with the monks during the day and sat in Zen meditation at night. Even now in the Southern Hill he emphasized the importance to the practitioner of a combination of labor in the fields and Zen.

On this point, another monk and hermit in the Southern Hills, the great Zen scholar Xuyun spent 100 years emphasizing the relationship between practice and hewing wood and drawing water, cultivating the fields and growing one's own food.

Back in the hut in the Southern Hills, Nanshan Sanren took out everything that could be given away. From a pocket he produced some transparent colored stones, these were agate which somebody had brought back from Outer Mongolia and presented to him. He gave them all away to someone else. Others were given medicinal herbs or tea. He was finally left with several bottles of wine. One evening he invited me to sit down at the stone table while he went to the kitchen and cooked several dishes of wild herbs which he brought to the table. Several workers repairing the hut were also invited to drink with us. He had been preparing this since the previous year. As we drank, Sanren described his own faults over the last few years, he had always been hot-tempered, people knew that he swore and could be violent. There had been people who wanted to stay overnight at the hut who were happy to eat but not to work in the fields and he would throw them out in a rage. He said that he should really go right into the hills, face a wall and contemplate his faults. Moreover, there were not many people who really needed him at the moment, when the day came when somebody was ill and needed a doctor and the doctor was ill beyond hope of recovery, then perhaps that would be the time to return to the crowd. More important was the fact that he liked living with the squirrels, beasts and birds in the depths of the mountains where there was no food, no house, no tea and no need to speak.

Next morning, early, when the mist over the roof had not yet cleared, we accompanied Sanren on his way into the hills. Sanren had engaged Lao Wu, an old friend, to go with him. Lao Wu was a little older than Sanren, he had his own business in town but believed that there was nothing of significance apart from practice. Once having met Sanren he was willing to follow him into the hills and live in a cave and eat pine needles. Master Sun, having heard several days previously that Sanren was returning to the hermetic existence, had rushed back from Hubei to see him off and Master Li who had come and passed Sanren's examination the previous year was to be the new occupant of the hut.

Before going into the hills Sanren had sat down and discussed things with his girlfriend. Sanren hoped that she would leave and go down the mountain to lead her own life, he didn't want her to turn into primitive man, her physique was not strong enough. However, she reacted strongly and what she said had to persuade him to take her with him into the hills. She said, do you believe that you are the only one who can live in a cave and eat pine needles? Why have you not asked me whether I like life off the mountain or not?

I had never seen Sanren's companion so agitated before.

Before setting out, Master Li had prepared some Solomon's

seal and Jade bamboo seeds and a vine root. Sanren himself carried a hoe, Master Li insisted on taking an axe. I didn't know how far they were going. Sanren lead the way without looking back at the hut where he had lived for ten years.

When he had first arrived the place had been a grave-yard. He had slept in a tree at night and there had been a bear's den close-by. During the day he had cleared stones to make a waterway and when hungry had eaten pine needles, the inexhaustible food of practitioners in the Southern Hills for thousands of years. Lacebark and horsetail pines grew in profusion in the valley close to the hut and later a number of daoist admirers had joined the procession of hut builders and brought provisions as well. They had propped up a metal basin on stones, lit a fire and cooked wild herbs and porridge, one practitioner had wept when he tasted the wild herbs. Ten years had passed, the roof of the hut was now sprouting grass but it was as solid as ever, perhaps it would give shelter to even more lay people but it was no longer secluded.

We started our trek into the depths of the mountains from the hill behind the hut, we had left in such a hurry that I had no time to take any luggage or a pack. In the period leading up to the departure to live in seclusion Sanren had taken Master Li into the hills to find a suitable spot. They had set off before the mist had cleared in the morning and had returned in the small hours. Sanren said that they had found a hill valley where there was a depression at the peak of a mountain, there was only one way into the valley through a waterfall surrounded by precipices. He still planned to go there, it was probably situated not far from Taiyi Peak in the Southern Hills at about 2,600 meters above sea level.

We set out southwards along a track trodden by both climbers and bears and about two hours later paused to rest by a spring where we picked up some abandoned mineral water bottles, washed them out and filled them with spring water for the journey. Sanren led us, climbing up a dried out water course towards a hill valley.

It was already May but the pine trees had not shed last year's needles. In the shade of the steep valley, the frozen soil was beginning to melt exposing lumps of ice. This was the kind of valley that climbers feared, there was not a trace of a path but Sanren scrambled forward over the rocks in the river valley like a monkey. Master Sun started to slow down, he had been coughing all the way and sometimes could not catch his breath. Master Li was the same. Perhaps Master Sun had spent too long in a daoist temple and had not walked in the hills for a number of years. I shouldered the pack that Master Sun had been carrying and the column moved slowly forward towards the even steeper part of the valley, in some places we were surrounded by mud as we helped each other forward. In one particularly precipitous hollow the stream appeared at long last, going underground further down the valley and flowing out over a cliff as a waterfall. A crag projected into the air beneath the waterfall with the sun dancing over the tips of luxuriant grass. We didn't want to go on any longer and dropped down beneath the pine trees in the wood. There was a withered birch tree on the steepest rock by the waterfall and Sanren told us to look up and see the *lingzhi* fungus growing all over it. The sight restored my energy immediately and I was the first to volunteer to go and pull some down. The rock that led to the tree was dripping with water. My clothes were soaked as I climbed it and then climbed the tree to pull down some fungus. The fungus was black and I scraped my hand on the surface of the rock as I scrambled down. It was difficult to stop the bleeding but I applied some kneaded earth and soon forgot it.

Sanren said that we could gather even more fungus on this

route so we should not go hungry. There were more and more azaleas as we climbed and even in winter you could see a sea of flowers, the trees higher up were greener than those lower down. Spring this year seemed to have been much later than usual but in the hills the climate is favorable throughout the year. Once past the steep waterfall the upper valley gradually opened out and we gathered more fungus from dried out tree stumps. Sanren's girlfriend found a fungus the size of a washing bowl in a pile of stones. In the end, as the fungi we were now gathering were larger and larger we left the smaller fungi to the mountain gods.

Once through the valley we climbed a ridge and there were more and more of the azaleas that Sanren had mentioned, however, the flowering season was already over and all that could be seen were the handsome dark green leaves. It was fine in the sunshine on the ridge and Master Sun and Master Li's coughs had disappeared. We sat at the edge of a cliff in the wind from the empty valley and Sanren's girlfriend produced biscuits and dates from her pack, some for everybody, this was our lunch. The sun was now in the west and we still wanted to rest but Sanren urged us on. We passed through a pine wood and the ridge broadened out as we went. Sanren said that this was a mountain meadow of the Qinling range. Through a patch of silver birches and suddenly a panorama of feathered bamboo opened up into the distance, the mountain meadow extended along the ridge further to the west. Through the meadow and we were in Zhashui county, we pushed through patch after patch of silver birch and feathered bamboo where the ivy arum seemed to have been growing for over a hundred years and was thicker than the trunks of the birch trees. At dusk we walked westwards along the ridge towards the setting sun. My face and hands had been scratched amongst the feathered bamboo and the others were no exception. In order to avoid

167

being submerged and lost in this vast forest of feathered bamboo, Sanren finally suggested that we should stop and have something to eat.

Another pack of biscuits and dates appeared from Sanren's girlfriend's pack. Having divided it into several stomach cheating portions, I glanced casually at that knapsack loaded with supplies. It was too small, it couldn't possibly contain our next meal.

In the distance, there were no more high mountains. In the west there was a range of light blue hills which should be Mount Taiyi, further west, out of sight, was the highest peak of the Southern Hills, Mount Taibai. Sanren said that he had felt long ago that there were hermits living in this uninhabited area. Attracted by this topic everybody had gathered round, very much interested in the other-worldly personages that Sanren had met in his ten years in the hills. Sanren said that several years ago he had run out of food and had therefore taken work as a laborer on a work-site in the hills. One day, a daoist priest had appeared at the site just as the workers were taking a rest-break, the priest had walked through the crowd of people towards him and they had smiled in mutual recognition but had not spoken. However, none of the other people on the work-site had seen the priest. Sanren said that to have reached this state of practice could be said to be the achievement of the way. Those with virtue were like a goose that flew across the sky and left no trace.

We pushed on before darkness fell, following Sanren towards the place that he sensed within him. We crossed ridge upon ridge, several times finding ourselves on the edge of a precipice in the darkness of the woods but we had reason to believe that Sanren could lead us to our destination. He never seemed to tire and marched at the front and in places where there were wild boar or bear tracks he had to remove a large number of land mines. They had been buried in the woods with their copper fuses smeared in sesame oil. He carefully scooped the mines out of the ground and buried them in a deeper pit, thus depriving some ingenious hunter of the opportunity of making a fortune.

Despite our fatigue, we were a long way from any populated place and if anybody couldn't manage, we all had to stop. Darkness gathered and it seemed as if we would never be out of the forest. Sanren never stopped and was sometimes too far ahead, we could only shout and then he quickly returned to the rescue.

It was only when we discussed where we would camp for the night that we discovered that we had drunk all the water in our bottles. There was no trace of water on the ridge and we decided to go south, find a valley and camp only when we had found a source of water. The night birds called and the wind rose in the forest and the bamboos knocked against each other as if performing a piece of heavenly music. I believed there was nobody who had the heart to enjoy it because the further we went the more at a loss we seemed to be. It was dark and difficult to see where to tread and the foliage returned to its original position when the person in front passed through. An hour later we stopped and sat in the undergrowth mopping our sweat and holding our breath as we tried to make out the sound of water around us. In the wind it was difficult to distinguish the soughing of the wind in the pines from the sound of water in the valley. Sanren insisted upon leading us deeper into the valley and we soon felt mud underfoot, we were closer and closer to a source of water. I didn't know where the water started from and then suddenly a small clear sounding stream appeared in front of us and the more the valley broadened the more the water thundered. We had found a river at last.

We dropped our packs to make camp at a place where we

▲ A hermit listening to the wind (Photo/Zhang Jianfeng)

could just make out the path. Water was a hand's reach away. Master Li took a metal basin from his pack and prepared to make a fire to boil water whilst Lao Wu and I searched for firewood. We soon found some large withered trees. Sanren cleared a space and we brought stones and branches, built benches and sat round a camp-fire. Apart from Sanren and myself, all the others produced groundsheets and sleeping bags from their packs in a kind of conjuring trick. Sanren's girl-friend draped a cloak used for seated Zen over his shoulders. We huddled together in a tired mass wrapped in sleeping bags and I saw my shadow like a round hedgehog in the dancing flames. The ground was frozen and our shoes were still wet from our trek. We roasted our shoes as we boiled the fungus we had collected. I sat in anticipation, not knowing how the fungus would taste but willing to eat it to fill my stomach.

Hunger would not wait too long for the fungus to cook and

we drank the fungus soup from the bowl in turn. It may not have been boiled long enough and I was greatly disappointed by the taste. When we had finished, Sanren looked at us and laughed and then, as a pleasant surprise, produced five packets of instant noodles from his pack, one each, except for himself.

Using two twigs as a pair of chopsticks I polished off the bowl of noodles and soup, the first time I've felt good about instant noodle junk food.

I couldn't help feeling excited at squatting round a camp-fire at night for the first time. Apart from Lao Wu and myself the others were soon snoring. In the latter half of the night the moon rose from behind the hills in the east and I entered the world of dreams.

Putting out the fire next morning Sanren said that during the night, somebody had approached in the dim moonlight and beckoned to him. We asked each other and nobody had got up in the night. What Sanren said cast an eerie atmosphere over the valley.

As he scooped up ice-cold water that chilled to the bone to wash his face, Sanren suggested that we should continue to follow this valley in search of the ideal but unlocated valley. We discovered several plastic bags by the stream, clearly this was a place within reach of the backpackers of the Southern Hills. The valley broadened out as we went and if we continued downstream we might reach one of the towns in the south. Although I dearly loved this forest moment I was actually beginning to feel nostalgia for the sweet food given in alms in the towns.

When the sun shone into the valley we stopped where it broadened out and lit a fire to boil some water, shared out the final few packets of instant noodles and then unzipped the sleeping bags for a short nap. Sanren had planned to return to the original ridge and move towards the range of hills in the

171

east, now he could only attempt to reach the ring-shaped valley above the waterfall that he had discovered last time. As we set out again, we saw that Master Li's face had turned green. He never spoke much and just as we were about to reach the ridge once more he fell far behind the column and then just fell and vomited in the undergrowth. The column had to stop. Sanren took a look and relating his symptoms to his former life-style, said that this was a cumulation of pre-existing illnesses, the food he cooked was always heavily flavored, it was too strong.

After a rest, Sanren cleared out Master Li's pack of everything except what was needed at the destination, such as copies of the sutras. The *lingzhi* fungus and paper products were discarded. Perhaps Master Li did not have the strength for a kilo more of weight. With the sun overhead we crossed valley after valley and only found a small valley spring at noon. We had finished our food, my legs were beginning to ache from all the walking and once on the level Master Sun and I sat down on the grass to rest hoping to hear Sanren say we would go no further so that we could then relax.

At dusk, having crossed at least ten valleys, we entered another valley. Sanren shouted with excitement and we finally heard him say that he had found it. The breathless Master Li's spirits rose, they both recognized this as a valley they had visited before. The sun was down in the west, it was getting dark, tall birch trees covered the valley but nobody was interested in the fungus in the trees. At the side of a wide stream Sanren led the search for that mysterious ravine, the stream became more and more choked and Sanren paused beside a steep waterfall. After resting, we clambered up through a crevice of rocks and undergrowth alongside the waterfall on the last stretch of the mountain path and at the top of a massive blue boulder a gorge appeared.

It was an oval valley shaped like a vase formed from solid

rock. It was covered in bamboo and some unknown trees. The river flowed through the center of the valley and turned into a waterfall at the top of the cliff.

Beside the river, Sanren found a cliff, amidst remnants of ice, that would give shelter from the rain. He planned to make it his sleeping place. Before dark we cut and gathered a large quantity of feathered bamboo and laid it over the ice, planning to sleep there overnight and to make a camp-fire close to the cliff. By the time we finished laying the bedding, Lao Wu was already making fungus soup and had added some pine needles. This time, we had the patience to wait until the soup boiled. After dark, a strong wind started to blow in the valley, the stars danced in the sky and we each chose a pillow from a pile of stones. Some of us couldn't wait to drink the fungus soup and go to sleep. Lao Wu left the camp-fire to go to the toilet and suddenly discovered that he hadn't brought any toilet paper with him. Just as he was thinking that this was a serious problem Master Li gave him a strip of birch bark. We laughed and wondered whether his skin would be able to take the roughness of the bark.

Master Li had been born in the Daxing'anling mountains in the north east where silver birches grew profusely. He suggested that Lao Wu could boil the birch bark in water to produce not only environmentally friendly toilet paper but writing material as well. He had once used birch bark as a medium for traditional Chinese painting.

As I drifted off to the land of dreams Lao Wu was still attending to the fungus soup beside the fire. Early next morning the fire had gone out and the soup was covered in wood ash. It had rained overnight and we were half-soaked and shivering with cold. After a wash, Master Li, Master Sun and I prepared to go back down the mountain.

Sanren enthusiastically described his new plans. He would

plant the whole area beside the stream with Solomon's seal and Jade bamboo as his winter food supply. He might also take charge of his girl friend and Lao Wu and slowly build a stone hut to live in. Lao Wu would have to become accustomed to a daily diet of fungus and pine needles and using birch bark as toilet paper. These possibilities presented no problem to his girlfriend, in the years that she had been with Sanren she had turned from a young woman into a practitioner. During the last two days of trekking, like Sanren, she had left us far behind.

When we emerged from the valley, peach and apricot blossom blazed from the roadside and the spring rain drifted across the hills. I had no idea how Sanren would manage to sleep in the rain.

He would no longer need financial support, there would be nobody to ask him about useless   subjects such as how old he was and how long he had lived in the mountains.

I met Lao Wu again about two months later. I was astonished to see that he was a different person. He was much thinner, he had a gentle expression and he no longer showed off in conversation. In those two months they had built a stone hut with their own hands, as well as a tree-house of branches that nested in a tree opposite the river.

After Sanren had left the straw hut in the Southern Hills, a lay person from Henan came to call on him and insisted that Master Li should take him deep into the mountains to see him. On the return journey he fell over a cliff and the rescue squad took a day to extricate him, fortunately he was not fatally injured. From then on, one heard very little of people going in to the mountains to call on Nanshan Sanren.

When it rains, I stand, off mountain, at a south-facing window looking towards the Southern Hills in the distance. Perhaps Nanshan Sanren is sitting on a rock under the waterfall singing that daoist song …

Chapter Six

The Land of the Investiture of the Gods

Hermits have had a hidden relationship with the Chinese people since ancient times. Nearly 1,500 years after the Yellow Emperor asked Guangchengzi, who was living as a hermit in the upper reaches of the Wei River, about Daoism, another hermit called Jiang Ziya (c. 1156 BC — 1017 BC) was living in seclusion in the Southern Hills. The classic Chinese novel of the supernatural *The Investiture of the Gods* (*Fengshen Bang*) describes how, on the instructions of his master, The Lord of Primordial Beginning, Jiang Ziya descended from the hills to assist an alliance led by the Western Zhou tribe to overthrow the Shang emperor and how, in a great battle of gods and men, he created 365 other deities. Jiang Ziya lived in solitude on the Pan River about 10 kilometers from the ancient place of Xiqi. King Wen of Zhou led a party to seek him out, appointed him to the highest positions and with his help destroyed the Shang dynasty. At the age of 139, this most famous of the hermits in Chinese history left his mortal remains on the banks of the Wei River and returned to the land of the immortals. Confucians, Daoists, Legalists and the Military School[1] all regarded him as a great teacher. Even today people believe that it was he who

---

1 One of the many philosophical schools of the Spring and Autumn and Warring States periods—*Trans*

defined almost all the tutelary deities.

Today the Pan River valley is known as the Diaoyutai Scenic Area and is at Guozhen in the Baoji municipality, Shaanxi province. It flows from the Qingfeng hills west of Mount Taibai and joins the Wei River 20 kilometers downstream. With my photographer colleague Guo Feng I planned first to find Practitioner Sun, living as a hermit amongst the people in Baoji and then to go up the Pan River to visit the great Jiang Ziya.

At Practitioner Sun's home beside the Wei River we found many of the classics handed down by the famous figures of Chinese mythology, as well as records of ancient systems of practice that we had never heard of. From a great pile of books Practitioner Sun produced a volume of the Manual of the Heavenly Whip handed down by Jiang Ziya as well as texts of the classics of the imaginary and actual religions in *The Investiture of the Gods*. Common sense prevented me from accepting that such rare books could so surprisingly be concentrated in the hands of a single person. This gave me reason to think that 3,000 years ago there must have been many more sources of culture and that these cultures slowly converged with the streams of daoist culture but still flowed like an underground river in folk culture thereby nourishing China's mainstream culture.

In Practitioner Sun's eyes, traditional Chinese culture resembled the five elements[1] and the five flavors. He said that you could not taste just one of the flavors of sour, sweet, bitter, spicy and salty. Amongst these flavors, salt represented the gentleman and possessed the hermetic spirit, any dish needed the addition of salt but, in the end, did not taste of salt. It

---

1 Wood, fire, earth, metal and water—*Trans*

was only after the blending together of Chinese cultures that philosophical schools of thought had emerged. The practices of traditional cultures had been handed on in a continuity that had never been broken. Within folk culture itself, there had been people who had quietly handed on the most secret traditions of the Chinese people, very often they had been fisherman, woodcutters, peasants or ordinary self-made scholars.

Practitioner Sun's teacher had been a hermit from Sichuan. A collection of thousands of ancient Chinese texts were kept by folk hermits. For over ten years he had travelled to most of the villages of north China to collect them. He said that if we were not going up the mountain we could take a couple of bags of books back with us.

That night we stayed at a small hotel called the Panxi Palace still 20 kilometers from the Pan River. Just over five kilometers to the north was the place where Qiu Chuji had lived as a hermit. Eight hundred years ago, having mourned for three years at the grave-side of Wang Chongyang, the founder of the Complete Truth School, Qiu Chuji had come to the Pan River, his aim as a hermit being to refine his own nature. Always fond of bustle and excitement and leaving aside the basic conditions required for living, the first problem a hermit faces is how to overcome the solitude in his heart. Here, Qiu Chuji wrote the poem:

With bitter passion for unpeopled space,
Flying high I escape the cage.
Empty days pass in poetry,
Watching the changing wind.
Staff in hand I climb from south to north,
And in drunken song from west to east.
Nothing of the reddened dust
Can reach those clouds of white.

Every day in his six years by the Pan River as a hermit he carried someone across the river. A daoist classic records that: "Having neither basket nor ladle he begged a single meal a day by the Pan River, at night he slept without benefit of a mat. He wore a coat of straw and a bamboo hat both in winter and summer and people called him 'Mr Strawcoat-Bamboohat'".

After leaving the Pan River, Qiu Chuji continued westwards and lived as a hermit at Longmendong (Dragon's Gate Cave) for seven years. Thereafter, at the invitation of Genghis Khan he travelled thousands of miles with his disciples through present-day Kazakhstan and Uzbekistan to the snow clad mountains of Afghanistan. At the time Genghis Khan's army occupied both Asia and Europe. Genghis asked Qiu Chuji how he could live forever. Qiu Chuji told him that there was no avoiding death but that it was possible to extend life. The secret was a pure heart, absence of desire and abstaining from slaughter. Genghis approved his views and changed his own practice of large scale massacre in warfare. Once having occupied large areas of central and southern China he had previously planned to slaughter the inhabitants and turn the fields back to pasture. After obtaining Genghis Khan's approval and support, Qiu Chuji was able to secure the release of 30,000 Chinese and Jurchens whom Genghis Khan had enslaved, as well as a large number of Chinese scholars.

Sometime after six and having passed through villages and fields of blossoming rapeseed we stood at the entrance to the Jiang Zhiya Fishing Platform Scenic Area. The Pan River was held back by a large wall and all that could be seen were the blue hills beyond. The Pan River was almost as I had imagined it, a place of solitude, apart from the sound of waves and the light on the water there was only tranquility. In autumn, the surface of the water boils with mist and the cry of birds swirls the air currents to into a light breeze. I would just as soon live here and take work as a road sweeper.

I finally threw down my rucksack when we found the stone from which Jiang Ziya had fished. I might not be able to become a hermit in the mold of Jiang Ziya but I could at least use the scenery as a means of observing myself. There were two depressions in the rock, about an inch deep worn smooth by kneeling, left it is said, by Jiang Ziya himself. On a cliff near the fishing stone was an inscription which read: "The blue cliff bears a print, the best are caught without a hook." [1]

This is a stream that has its place in any number of moral tales, although there is no great expanse of water and it can't really be called a river. That has had no effect on the fact that it has nourished the spirit of countless Chinese. Where the river widens, there stands a towering rock known as "the *pu* kept in the *huang*". Tradition has it that this several hundred ton rock was hooked from the belly of a fish by Jiang Ziya. The four-character inscription from which the rock takes its name was carved in the Qing dynasty. *Huang* is an uncut stone that contains jade and *pu* is a nearly finished jade vessel. Fishing in the Pan River, Jiang Ziya caught a *huang* and was invited by King Wen to become the teacher of the state and to assist King Wu of Zhou in the task of unification. Nevertheless, there were still many hermits in the population, of whom people never knew, who were unwilling to be discovered or who were not discovered.

There was a three-roomed temple next to the huge rock containing a statue of Jiang Zhiya and I went in to pay a call on this hermit of three thousand years ago. The temple keeper was a typical inhabitant of Guanzhong. He was unselfconsciously

---

1 A reference to the legend that Jiang Ziya fished with a straight hook upon which "only the willing could be caught", a technique which attracted the attention of King Wen and caused him to engage Jiang Ziya—*Trans*

practicing calligraphy on an old newspaper. I asked him about local conditions and he said that the four leaning cypresses in front of the temple were 1,300 years old, they represented the sun, moon, stars and time. There were three halls to the temple, closely connected with the three realms of Daoism. On the precipice above the narrow valley there was a "hall of tranquility" where Jiang Ziya the fisherman had lived. He had lived in that tiny cave for over ten years.

He much preferred reading, sleeping and practicing calligraphy to talking to people. When I left I wanted to know his name, the reply I received was "Man of the Mountains and Fields".

Mount Taibai, situated 3,800 meters above sea-level, is the birthplace of ancient Chinese mythology. It is covered in snow all year round and extends for several hundred *li*, taking in the counties of Zhouzhi, Meixian and Mount Taibai itself. The range stretches westwards to the Longmen (Dragon's Gate) Caves, Mount Kongdong and the snow covered Kunlun Mountains. Gulouguan is less than 20 *li* to the east and continuing east along the range are Mount Huashan and Mount Song. To the south is Mount Wudang. This is the earliest area in which the ancient daoists were active.

Historically there were numerous mountain deities on Mount Taibai but they shared the common characteristic of the maintenance of moral integrity and aspiration; as Kongzi (Confucius) put it: "If I heard the way in the morning then I may die easy at dusk." The ancient Chinese regarded death both as a sublimation and explanation of the way and personal integrity. I thought of the gods of Mount Taibai, they were certainly mutually self-aware, they lay smiling in the haze gazing at the disillusion of the red dust, as if watching so many mayflies dreaming on the water.

Worshippers and tourists can only reach the top of Mount

▲ On Mount Taibai (Photo/Guo Feng)

Taibai in June and July each year, when the several way-stations on the mountain have people who can supply food, padded clothing and accommodation to travelers. Climbing the mountain in other seasons requires you to carry your own tent and sleeping bag, generally an ascent of the mountain takes three days.

In April there is nobody on the mountain because of the weather. We enquired everywhere about hermits living on the mountain, the answers were disappointing. Nobody could say definitely that there were practitioners on the mountain. Some said that there were several daoist priests living at the Tiejiashu (Armor Tree) Temple on the southern slopes, nobody could live higher up but I heard from frequent travelers on the mountain that many years previously someone had been living as a hermit in a cave on Mount Taibai in a place that

▲ Practitioners by the Hei River below Mount Taibai (Photo / Guo Feng)

was inaccessible to ordinary people. I was too liable to become enthusiastic on the vaguest evidence, a habit shared by many others.

There was only one morning bus a day from the Zhouzhi County bus depot to the southern slope of Mount Taibai. We missed it and had to shoulder our packs and sigh at the hills, moved by the strength of leg of the ancients. It was several hundred *li* to Houzhenzi, our destination and faced by the four wheels of a bus we lost confidence in our two feet.

Our search would start in Zhongnanzhen, the only town off mountain that takes its name from the Southern Hills (Zhongnanshan). In ancient times this was a way-station for hermits going up into the mountains, tradition has it that several daoist priests had practiced here for many years.

We asked an old fruit seller about the whereabouts of daoist temples and based on his directions very easily found a dilapidated temple whose buildings looked "pre-Cultural Revolution". The courtyard was filled with seated old ladies who warmly invited us to take a drink of water. We met the priest in charge of the temple who had lived there for five years and very rarely left its precincts. He said that his only task was to supervise the burning of incense even though very few people actually came to light incense. He suggested that we should go to Doucun (Bean Village) and find the daoist priest Sun. As we left the temple the seated old ladies stood and sent us on our way with a daoist salutation. Their expression was as friendly as a grandmother's.

As if to prove a relationship with beans, the fields round Doucun were almost all planted with them, their flowers a pure snow white. We asked an old man after Priest Sun's temple, he looked us up and down and said you've asked the right person, in this village I'm the one who knows most about Daoism. Since we've come to visit Daoism he went on—and excitedly recommended us to several hermits who lived by the Mount Shouyang and then left.

We met an elderly daoist priest on the road not far from the temple we were searching for. He looked full of vigor and I thought he ought to be the man we were seeking. Just as I had expected, Priest Sun said that his temple was not far ahead, he was on his way back. He did not have the key with him and he was waiting for somebody to bring it over.

He had lived here for over ten years. It was not far from where he had been born. He said that his task was to solve people's concrete requirements. Many people came looking for him when they were sick, he did not employ herbal remedies, patients' problems could be solved by talking to them. If they needed him to do something then he did it. We asked him how it was that he looked so relaxed. He said there was no secret, just eating and sleeping. Normally, there was not much going on and he didn't go out of his way to find things to do. All he did was to pass the days of actual life in a carefree way. He had no desire to be an immortal. It was enough just to live.

The village street was filled with the blossom of the tung-tree and the breeze that blew from the Southern Hills wafted the sweet scent of sprouting wheat across the fields. We were anxious to get back to Zhouzhi county to catch the early bus towards Mount Taibai the next day and said goodbye to Priest Sun.

Early next morning the bus to Houzhenzi looked like a village on the move, almost everybody knew each other and the conversation in the bus was about household topics. People were squeezing on to the bus throughout the journey so that the inside of the bus much resembled a compressed package. I kept on straining my neck to get some fresh air. It took the bus four hours to travel from the pass into the mountains to Houzhenzi where it finally discharged us with a sigh. We exchanged our feet for a motorbike which took us to the Armor Tree Temple. This was one of the better daoist temples on the southern slopes of Mount Taibai and took its name from a 3,000 year old armor tree (*nageia fleuryi*).

There was no wall round this temple. A practitioner squatted under the armor tree as if he had been waiting for us for a long time. The title he had given himself was Free as Mist. When we explained why we had come, he shouted towards the woods on the river bank and a voice responded from across the river. In a little while the daoist priest Sun appeared before us, he had been in the woods gathering herbs. Priest Sun said that rumor had it that there was a city built of white stone in the mountains and that people who had the right affinity would be able to find its entrance, it was the city of the immortals.

Priest Sun was a disciple of Ren Xingzhi, the abbot of the Louguantai Daoist Monastery. The Armor Tree Temple had been a part of the Louguantai monastery from early on and

▲ A hut on Mount Taibai (Photo / Guo Feng)

many of the daoist priests from the monastery visited it for meditation. A vertical Chinese bamboo flute and two chess sets were in Priest Sun's room. He had been here for five years but it was Priest Li who had been here the longest.

Priest Sun showed us into a smoke blackened room of mud brick. Priest Li was asleep. A dragon-headed walking stick and a broadsword leant against the brick *kang* sleeping platform. A moment later he sat up on the *kang* and asked whether we were going exploring? His tone softened when we greeted him with clasped hands. I said that we had come to enquire about the way. He laughed and said he only had wine.

Priest Li very much resembled Li Kui, the Black Whirlwind, a character from the classical novel the *Water Margin*. He

185

was dressed in a black daoist robe and his large eyes looked electric. Fifty years earlier he had become a daoist at Mount Wudang and had lived in seclusion on the rear slopes of Mount Wudang for over ten years studying martial arts. For the last decade or so he had mainly studied herbal medicine. Priest Sun added that he was also an alchemist and I immediately thought of the elixir of life. I noticed the several tens of large and small bags hanging from the rafters containing herbs that Priest Li had gathered in the mountains. He said that at the time and in order to achieve the highest realms of medical practice, Sun Simiao (c. 581 – 682) the "King of Medicine" himself had borrowed some land from the god of Mount Taibai to grow medicinal herbs. The god had given him the land that surrounded Yaowangdian (Hall of the Medicine King) up to a distance of several tens of *li*. There was not a single weed on the mountain. A record could be found of every plant in medical texts. There were 98 varieties of pseudo-ginseng (*sanqi*) together with Taibai rice, Taibai plum, Taibai tea and stellera, triponium tuber and other rare plants.

Two days earlier Priest Li's disciple, who also planned to live in seclusion on the mountain, had been up the mountain looking for a site. There was a practitioner living in seclusion above Sanhegong who had arrived three years ago but nobody had seen him. He had heard that his standard of cultivation was quite high.

Two days' march further up the mountain was Yuhuangchi (Jade Emperor's Pool) where one did not speak in a loud voice lest the sound brought down a hailstorm from the clouds. In the mountains the wind was known as "weiwei" and if you spoke this word you would soon know how serious the consequences could be. A daoist priest lived at Yuhuangchi, a disciple of the female daoist who had restored the Armor Tree Temple before he had taken over. She had lived on the mountain for fifty years and had suffered much hardship. She now lived somewhere else.

I asked Priest Li his reasons for living here for so many years. He replied why should there be so many reasons?

Here, time did not exist. Every day was the same, drinking wine and sleeping at night and gathering herbs when he had the leisure. He had once aspired to the higher realms of medicine, now it was just drinking. Priest Sun produced a bottle of herbal wine from the corner of the room with some ginseng roots in it, each root had grown for several hundred years. Have a drink! Priest Li said one's life was like a shower of rain and a bit of cloud, and all was well.

After we had had a drink he produced some herbal drugs for us to identify while Priest Sun drew a bucket of water from the river in front of the temple and started to cook. The evening meal was stir-fried cabbage, *mantou* and gruel, just what I fancied.

Free as Mist was disappointed on our behalf, had we arrived two day earlier we would have been able to eat a kind of delicious tasting flower that blossomed on a tree. It only blossomed for three days and was difficult to pick. I gave thanks inwardly to the god of Mount Taibai for the meal that he had prepared for us and started to deal with the great pile of *mantou* in front of me. Priest Li continued drinking. They said that for over ten years he had only drunk wine and basically abstained from cereals. He could drink several catties of wine a day. Recently the bottom of the wine barrel had appeared so he had drunk less.

Once we had finished eating Priest Li sat on the *kang* to meditate while we sat under the armor tree and chatted to Free as Mist against the background of the music of the river. There was an indefinable scent of plants in the air, coming from nowhere and going I know not whither, sometimes present and sometimes not.

▲ A practitioner beneath Mount Taibai (Photo/Guo Feng)

Free as Mist pointed out a large rock, the place where Priest Li slept and practiced, most of the time he was drinking or he was to be found asleep on the rock.

Free as Mist's family was off mountain. For many years he had wanted to study under Ren Farong, the daoist priest at the Louguantai Daoist Monastery. However Priest Ren had believed that there was a murderous look to him and that he should wait and cultivate himself much more and then think again. He had been waiting for very many years.

The temple was surrounded by hills and the river in front of it flowed down from the Dayehai Lake on the northern side of Baxiantai near the summit of Mount Taibai at a height of 3,590 meters. Dayehai is a classic frozen lake comparatively well preserved and dating from the fourth period of glaciation. The lake was still covered in ice and snow and would only start to melt in about a month's time. Looking carefully at the river in the sun, it seemed to be emitting wisps of frozen smoke. There was a profusion of wild flowers on the bank and the ground was carpeted with pine cones. I wanted to find someone to play chess with, using the stones in the river. Free as Mist then recited a line from the poet Su Dongpo: "Playing chess beneath the pines, suddenly the pine-needles fall like pieces of chess."

Free as Mist said that you could not drink water straight from the river, it was ice-cold. If you dipped your hand in the water, in a few minutes it would be numb. However it was ideal for making tea though few people drank tea hereabouts. They mostly drank potions of boiled pine needles or fairy reed (*Curculigo orchioides*).

Nightfall rose like mist from the floor of the valley and we went quickly to bed. Sometimes, by the light of the moon, takin or bears charged into the temple courtyard but Priest Sun had let loose the two temple dogs before we went to sleep and during the night they patrolled everywhere like bodyguards.

The next morning, not having prepared to sleep in the snow, we didn't climb to Baxiantai but after breakfast said a slow farewell to the mountain gods of Mount Taibai and to the armor tree. As we were about to leave Free as Mist wrote out one of Li Bai's poems on a sheet of fine paper and presented it to us:

Drinking face to face
Amidst the mountain blossom,
Cup upon cup
And then another.
I am drunk and need to sleep
And you must go,
But return tomorrow if you will,
And bring your *qin*.

Chapter Seven

A Home to Ravens

Mount Huashan has been the home of hermits since ancient times. It stands like a lotus with its roots in the red dust and its buds swaying above the mist and cloud. There are 72 caves on Mount Huashan. This daoist fairyland is the home of daoist hermits and acts as a conduit to another realm of space-time. Only those daoists who have achieved immortality can reach the immortals' true abode. Historically, many daoist hermits chose to live in caves deep in the mountains, remote and detached from the world, abstaining from grain and imbibing elixirs. They carved their texts on the walls of caves or hid their own writings in the crevices of rocks.

I believe that in a former life I had been a woodcutter in the depths of Mount Huashan where I felled trees in the boundless mists with hermits or sacred cranes as my constant companions. One day during the rainy season in the Southern Hills, Master Huang who lived on the upper reaches of the Dayu River came down the mountain and invited me to accompany him on an ascent of Mount Huashan with a daoist monk called Hao, thus avoiding the expensive entrance charge. Master Hao had lived for over ten years in a stone dwelling at the Qunxian Temple on Mount Huashan. He was an expert herbalist and had cured many people of chronic illnesses. The ancient daoists had all carried a gourd so that they could make up medicines wherever they went. Master Hao had merely exchanged his gourd for a cloth bag. He said that he had walked

▲ Mist on Mount Huashan (Photo/Zhang Jianfeng)

all over the hills round Mount Huashan to gather herbs. He had even visited the Zhongtiao Hills on the opposite bank of the Yellow River.

Master Hao's home was across the Yellow River in Shanxi. His father had been an expert on the *Book of Changes* and liked casting horoscopes for people. When he was born, a friend of his father's had said that, in a former life, he had been born in Weizhou during the Northern Wei dynasty and that he had had an affinity with Daoism and that the pattern of his life determined that he should become a monk at Mount Qingcheng. When he was in his teens he had learned the skills of a carpenter and had begun to earn his own living. However, things had not gone well and he had said goodbye to his parents and travelled from Shanxi, through Shaanxi to Sichuan in search of a teacher.

Whenever he had arrived in a place, he tried to find work as a carpenter to pay for his travel expenses. Sometimes, when his money was exhausted, he had begged in the streets. If he had nowhere to sleep at night he would go to a station waiting room but if he had no ticket he would be turfed out several hours later and that meant sleeping in the open. At Yangpingguan on the border between Shaanxi and Sichuan he had passed through three villages and hadn't received as much as a single *mantou* in alms. It was snowing and his clothing was threadbare. He eventually collapsed in the street with a fever. A woman from a small hostel had revived him with gruel and he had lain in the hostel for over three weeks before the fever had receded.

He had found a teacher for himself at Mount Laojun in Sichuan. Much heavy work had awaited him as a novice disciple. Every day during the winter he had had to trudge through the snow to break the ice and carry back water on a shoulder pole. He had also had to suffer the humiliations heaped on him by the other disciples. He said this was all part of the practice of the way.

His master had visited a number of men of talent on Mount Qingcheng, his master's teacher had been a disciple of the Jianxian (Immortal Sword) school of the Cave of the Heavenly Teacher, with a white beard to his chest, hale and hearty at the age of 100. According to one daoist priest he was one of the few existing swordsmen.

Master Hao showed us the *lingzhi* fungus he had gathered from the cliffs. He said that there was grass fungus and the stone fungus that grew in cliffs. Generally, people were only fortunate enough to be able to gather the *lingzhi* fungus that grew in earth. The fungus that grew on cliffs was luminous and usually unreachable. He said that herbs had a spiritual nature, mountain plants could escape as well. He had once put some polygonum to soak in a dish and it had disappeared when his back was turned.

Master Hao's stone hut had three rooms, the window looked out on mountain and white clouds and the precipice below, birds were not often to be seen. Before each journey off the mountain he always made up a batch of herbal pills.

There had been no guarantee of food and sleeping accommodation before he had arrived at Mount Huashan. Mount Huashan was one of China's famous scenic spots and the daoist monks who lived there permanently were appointed by the Daoist Association at the Yuquan Temple at the foot of the mountain. He had been sent to this spot and had been here for over ten years. Apart from the occasional journey off mountain to treat somebody's illness he had spent most of the time at this temple, it was his responsibility to look after it.

The construction of the Qunxian Temple took advantage of the cliff face, the rear wall of the great hall was formed by the white rock of Mount Huashan itself and a statue of the daoist spiritual master Lu Dongbin stood in a cave chiseled out of the wall. Master Hao rose at five o'clock every morning, his first task was to present a bowl of fresh water to Lu Dongbin and to burn incense and light candles in honor of this precursor who had achieved immortality on Mount Huashan.

Priest Huang and I were installed on a stone bed in a corner of the great hall and entered the land of dreams as we listened to the familiar sound of water dripping from the eaves.

There were not many tourists on the mountain during the autumn rain and very few were able to pause here to come and burn incense though the mountain mists were frequent visitors. The steps of the great hall descended into cloud, the mountain breeze passed through the pine forest playing a tune on the strings of the pine needle that only a hermit could understand, and the spring water ran in wrinkled eddies over

▲ A practitioner carrying up supplies on the rear slopes of Mount Huashan
(Photo/Zhang Jianfeng)

the white stones without speaking.

There had once been a band of immortals here but they had flown away on the backs of white cranes, looking at the vastness of the sky all around, nothing was to be seen of them, just the name Qunxian Temple—Temple of the Band of Immortals.

Master Hao said that there were over ten daoists who had been appointed by the Huashan Daoist Association to live permanently on Mount Huashan. Their supplies and necessities were carried up to them by porters hired by the association. Nevertheless, some practitioners who sought after tranquility thought that it was not peaceful enough and were always leaving Mount Huashan to live secluded in the remote places that tourists could not reach.

They might not need much food there, but it would require a deal of practice and cultivation, something that not all practitioners were able to achieve. Living in seclusion to cultivate the way signified moving completely beyond the world, totally abandoning all worldly entanglement and ideas of fame and profit, this was a long process. The cultivation of the way required one to pass through this stage before approaching the way itself. Although some had lived in seclusion for a life-time and had not reached the ultimate destination, the important point was that they were on the road that leads to it.

There were two caves which people were generally unable to reach on Mount Sangong across from the Changkong suspended plank pathway on the face of the cliff. The peaks of Mount Sangong were set out like the Great Bear, dangerous rocks standing like a forest with no definite path upwards, people rarely reached them.

Master Huang and I spent two nights on the stone bed at the Qunxian Temple. It poured with rain, I had wanted to take some photographs of the scenery of Mount Huashan, but like the wings of a crane the mist had obscured everything and photography had become a problem. We hadn't brought rainwear up with us, Master Hao rarely went out when it was wet and did not have bamboo hats or rush coats to lend us. We planned to stay for a few more days and return down the mountain after climbing to Luoyanfeng (Peak of the Falling Eagle) and visiting the Changkong suspended pathway.

Master Hao said that if I had an affinity for the immortals I might perhaps meet daoist Master Li Mingji, an adept living in seclusion on Mount Huashan. All the practitioners on Mount Huashan knew him and called him Li, the Great Immortal. Unfortunately he was not on the mountain at the moment, though I ought perhaps to go and see another, Master Wen, who lived at Jiutiangong (The Nine Heavenly Palaces). If I were lucky I might learn from him something of the great daoist of Mount Huashan. However, Master Wen was a man of uneven temper who spoke little. He had practiced the way with Master Li Mingji for many years at Wangdaoling (King's Way Ridge) opposite the main peaks of Mount Huashan.

Many years ago Master Hao had lived in the same temple on Mount Qingcheng as Master Li Mingji. Master Li had cared for him but at the time he had had too many attachments and his heart had not been in cultivating the way. With his own eyes he had once seen two pythons appear from he knew not where at the mouth of the cave where Master Li was living in abstinence and lie there unwilling to leave, he had been scared stiff. It was only later that he had discovered that the two snakes had been there to protect Master Li.

Master Hao said that he was normally unwilling to tell ordinary people about these things. They might not believe him. But in the practice of Daoism there was much that was beyond comprehension.

People who eat meat and fish everyday might well be attacked by wild animals when walking in the hills because they stank of fish, animals were able to distinguish such things. However, somebody who was pure in practice could walk in a mountain forest unharmed, the power of differentiation of an animal was no less than that of a human. If you were pure, animals appreciated your scent and would approach you.

Master Hao said that Master Li only returned to Mount Huashan in the winter. Normally he was wandering abroad treating illness. He didn't know where he was at present. He had heard that several months ago, he had been invited by a number of buddhist figures to give a public display of abstinence at the Tianjin Water Park lasting 57 days, during which he would only drink a little water. He had previously fasted in a cave for 81 days. After hearing what Master Hao

▶ The cave at Wangdaoling (Photo/Zhang Jianfeng)

had to say I thought that perhaps Master Li would be of some importance amongst the hermits that I was searching for in the Southern Hills.

A little after seven o'clock the following morning Master Huang and I climbed to the top of Luoyanfeng. The hill mist was like a cloud of dust, Master Huang came across a squirrel on a rock at the side of the path and named him Squirrel Friend of the Way. The squirrel stood watching us quietly from the top of the rock as if he had been on guard there for some time. Master Huang withdrew a chestnut from his daoist gown and left it for him. At the top of Luoyanfeng the sky was a brilliant blue, the sun had come out and where, beneath the clouds, the rivers Wei and Jing met the Yellow River, above a layer of grey smog it was a clear azure blue.

We sat down for a rest at Nantianmen below Luoyanfeng and a daoist nun invited us to take a drink of water. Her daoist title was Li Zhikun, and she came from the distant northeast. She said that this was the only temple on Mount Huashan that had daoist nuns, herself apart, there was her teacher Mother Jiang. For those visitors to Mount Huashan who liked exploring, this was the site of the entrance to its most dangerous Changkong suspended walk-way. The foot-wide walk-way lay out of the back door of the great hall of the temple and through a cave in the rock. Next to it was Juxiantai (Platform of the Assembled Immortals) suspended with air on three sides where, legend has it, the Yellow Emperor met the assembled immortals 5,000 years ago.

While Mother Jiang was resting, Li Zhikun took us to see the place where she collected water, a small rocky outcrop in mid-air with a green pool of water that was reached by a very narrow bridge of stone less than a palm's width wide and with a sheer drop on both sides.

She told me that the first time she had gone to collect

water with her teacher she had scrambled across astride and had not dared open her eyes. Later she had collected water early every morning. Mother Jiang was over 70 and to her it was like walking on level ground. Master Huang thought that he would try and see how sure-footed he was by walking across but was yelled at and told to go back by a nearby park ranger.

I merely had to look at it to make my head spin. When we returned from the edge of the precipice Mother Jiang was sitting in a corner of the great hall looking lean and vigorous.

She hadn't been off the mountain for over ten years. She told her disciple to give me the pine nuts that had been gathered from the trees a few days earlier to eat. Li Zhikun said that mother Jiang had picked these nuts while hanging over a precipice in a high wind. Mother Jiang had seemed as if swaying on the top of a wave as she perched on the tree branches. Li Zhikun had been so frightened that her feet had ached for days.

At our request Mother Jiang began to tell us how she came to Mount Huashan. Several decades previously she had put her family behind her and come to the foot of Mount Huashan to become a daoist. Her family found her and forced her to return home but later she ran away again. There had once been a local regulation banning daoist nuns from living on the mountain. She had climbed the mountain under cover of darkness and taken up residence in a cave beneath Dashangfang (The Upper Place) through which a stream ran. Even living deep in the mountain she feared discovery and only crept out of the cave at night to dig potatoes and pick eggplants from a nearby vegetable patch. She stole only a little each day, to have stolen more would have risked discovery. She lived in the cave undiscovered for three years until she was ill and at her last breath when she was discovered and rescued. She later secured the right to live here.

The situation was much better now, she said, and she could put all her heart into the practice of the way.

After saying goodbye to Mother Jiang we climbed the Chongkong suspended walk-way and after a section of path chiseled out of a precipice, the Chaoyuan Cave half hung over the cliff before us. The cave contained a statue of the great Yuan dynasty daoist adept, He Zhizhen (1212 – 1299). In the cave, a daoist priest with a long white beard was writing out the characters of the *Daodejing* with a brush. We knelt and burned incense before the statue of He Zhizhen. The keeper said that in this way the great master might protect us and prevent us from falling into the abyss.

Through the good offices of Master Huang my safety harness on the walk-way was free of charge. Despite the safety harness, I stepped cautiously in the howling wind, sticking to the cliff face like a gekko. Once finished with the walk-way, my hands ached because of the effort that I had used. The walk-way led to He's Old Cave, one that He Zhizhen and his two disciples had chiseled out on Mount Huashan in the Yuan dynasty and one of the 72 caves on the mountain.

The two disciples had been perplexed by the fact that their master taught them no doctrine at all and merely took them to dig out a cave each day. One day the disciples, bewailing their lack of luck, planned to follow this master no longer. The master was suspended over the cliff-face digging out the cave. From above they cut the rope that held him, thinking that since he liked digging out caves so much he had no need to come up again. Just as they were about to go down the mountain they looked back and saw that the master was still suspended from the rope, digging out the cave. They turned back at once to find him. They later became two of the many immortals of Mount Huashan.

Quanzhenya (the Cliff of Complete Truth) was above He's

Old Cave and I scrambled up through some trees above the cave and looked down, Master Huang and the nun Li Zhikun were sitting silently opposite each other under a tree by the cliff. The sun shone from above the opposite hills rendering the hills behind them a pale blue, they seemed to be beyond the sky. One day on the mountain was perhaps a hundred years below.

I had climbed half an hour through the cliff-top trees to catch this scene.

Back at Nantianmen Master Huang and I drank a bowl of Mother Jiang's tea and carried on to visit Master Wen at Jiutiangong.

Jiutiangong was in a ravine under the western peak of Mount Huashan, surrounded by mountains and with a blue stream as its neighbor. It was built with the elegance of a poem, the blue and cinnabar of the building matched by the white of the rock and the green blue shade of the trees, a sight fit for long-term contemplation.

Above the snow white steps of the courtyard several daoist monks were debating the various realms of practice. I enquired after the whereabouts of Master Wen of one of them who replied that he was Master Wen. He was not willing to say much about Master Li and suggested that I should ask another monk, Master Wang, who lived in a valley on the east of Mount Huashan about him. He had lived in a cave with Master Li for many years and was now looking after the cave at Wangdaoling for him.

Taking the large apple that Master Wen had presented us we bid farewell with clasped hands and carried on down the mountain. There was a court filled with artemisia alongside several ancient trees next to the Jiutiangong. It was impossible to judge its age from the walls but the huge stone arches in the courtyard made it look rather like a museum. Pushing open the mottled wooden door, the side rooms seemed as dark as

▲ Cave at the top of a precipice (Photo/Zhang Jianfeng)

night, a white bearded old daoist master emerged from the shadows of the interior and when he saw us, greeted us with a bow. He was full of the vigor of spring and said that he had lived here since after the Cultural Revolution, it had once been the Taihua Classical Academy.

About four hundred years ago, the great Guanzhong confucian scholar Feng Congwu (1556 – 1627), then Secretary of the Board of Works, had been unhappy at the power of the eunuchs at court and with the corruption at court and in government generally. He had been exiled to his home village where he had built the academy. He had also built another academy at Taiyifeng not far from Mount Huashan. Historically, after withdrawing from politics, many scholars chose to open schools and spend the remainder of their lives in education, perhaps a life of rural seclusion was the one most suited to those upright men.

It was the Maonu Cave below Qingkeping that I was anxious to visit. I found a notice at the entrance to the daoist temple below the Maonu Cave, the temple had merely borrowed the name of the cave. Looking up from the courtyard beneath the cave I could only see the snow-white rocks and green pines in the upper part of the valley and the custodian of the court said that it was almost impossible to reach the cave, it was outside tourist limits and, in any case, there was no road.

Parting at the gate we were a little deflated, thinking that this was a destiny that had not come to fruition. On down past the Maonu Cave was the Suoluo Level, and above that was the ravine where the famous daoist teacher Chen Tuan (871 – 989) had become an immortal.

I had described my plan of going into the ravine to find the spot where Chen Tuan had become an immortal to Master Hao before I came up into the hills. It is said that after entering a cave in the valley of Zhangchaogu, Chen Tuan told his disciples to seal its entrance with rocks. When, later, the disciples went to look for the cave the whole valley had collapsed. Master Hao said that very few people went there. There was no path anyway and it was also said that there were huge pythons in the valley. As it was raining my plan came to nothing but although I could not call on this hermit who lived in the depths of the clouds, it seemed as if the clear spring streams in the valley could act as a messenger between us. They originated in the clouds and flowed over the snow-white rocks and the moss of Mount Huashan. Where water was plentiful it was nearly green in color, where it was meagre there were just ripples and the color could not be made out. The streams had never been separated from the earliest hermits on Mount Huashan nor had space-time divided me from the hermits …

The tree ferns that Chen Tuan himself had planted had not waited for us either. They had gone with the river decades ago just leaving their name as a remembrance.

Opposite the Suoluo Level were some caves at the top of a cliff, the path to them was difficult to make out. We only found out from a souvenir seller at the side of the path that the path to Dashangfang and Xiaoshangfang went over the river in the valley and then up the cliff face. Try as I could I could not make out the location of Dashangfang. I'd heard that we had to go through a cave to get there. It was in that place beyond the imagination that Master Cao the former president of the Huashan Daoist Association lived, she was over 80. Her predecessor as president lived in the Cave Twelve by the Yuquan Temple and had died after the celebrations of his hundredth birthday.

In the river valley below the Suoluo Level, we saw a daoist priest with windswept hair and beard standing on a rock with his hands clasped behind him and a distant expression on his face, as if he were in another dimension of time and space. We did not disturb him and hurried on down the path towards the exit from the mountain.

It was already twilight when we saw the Yuquan Temple. Its construction was a miracle. It was almost built over the river in the valley. The trees in the courtyard were ancient and the stones were clean. The scent of trees and plants and the sound of the bell from the great hall reminded me that this was the home of the immortals.

Following the directions given us by Master Wen we crossed a bridge in the darkness and arrived at a cave in a certain valley on Mount Huashan. Daoist master Wang came out to welcome us. We told him the reason for our visit and he invited us in to his Yellow Dragon Cave to drink tea. His family came from Fujian. Over ten years ago he had set his mind on Mount Huashan, left his family and made his way here. He had been with Master Li continuously for eight years. He said that

▲ Li Mingji with his daoist friend at Wangdaoling (Photo/Zeng Dong)

his true daoist place was up in the mountains. He was only living here temporarily. Provided I possessed a sufficient sense of Daoism in my heart I might perhaps soon meet Master Li. Many people wished to meet him, it was a matter of the right moment. Master Wang said finally that in nearly 20 years of practice he had not met such a rare talent as Master Li.

I met Master Li several months later. He was as I had imagined, rather like an elderly urchin from a martial arts novel, a set of whiskers and when he talked as amusing as a child. He liked to accommodate people and lead them to the skills of abstinence. When they were unable to keep it up he would charge a "get out of here fee". He wanted everybody to be a friend and cared as much for the fame and profit that people pursued as for a cast off shoe.

I wanted to know who his master was, he said that he did too but these ten years past he had not been destined to meet him. After becoming a daoist at Mount Wudang he had gone to Qingyanggong in Sichuan and there had met a daoist priest who described himself as his daoist fellow student—entrusted by his master to instruct him in the way—he had been waiting there for over 80 days. Later he had lived in caves in the Tianshan and Kunlun mountains at over 4,000 meters above sea level for several years. He always liked to climb to caves that people could not reach in order to practice there. Master Li said that at the moment, for the expansion of the way, he was having to accustom himself to the scent of mankind and cure sickness in a city.

After meeting Master Li I thought I would go and see the cave where he practiced in seclusion. I followed the path I had taken last time back to Master Wang's Yellow Dragon Cave at the foot of Mount Huashan. Under his guidance I started the climb to Wangdaoling.

The route to Wangdaoling stretches for 17.5 kilometers. There were few people and the path twisted in and out of the steep valleys as the mountains became higher and higher. We pushed through thickets of thorn and saw a few lizards but no birds in flight. Three hours later we had left the smog covered plain and the floating clouds behind us. There was a solitary temple to the mountain god in the gorge and we rested on a bluish colored rock. Master Wang carried a new metal wok and some potatoes on a pole, for my part, I carried a few classics written by hermits. We drank the spring water from our flasks and eat some pine needles. I had left the apple as an offering to the mountain god.

There was a stream at the place from where Wangdaoling was visible and beside it a shepherd with his flock of 20 or more sheep and two dogs. We stopped at the shepherd's hut with its cooking smoke and he invited us in to drink tea. The

▶ Master Wang looking out from the "little square" at Wangdaoling (Photo/Zhang Jianfeng)

tea was bitter and made the stomach rumble. Afterwards we continued up the mountain and climbed to Wangdaoling as the sun sank towards the west.

At the top of a flight of stone steps there was a terrace beside a wood of mixed bamboo and lacebark pine. There was a hut built from piled stone with grass in front, with a moss covered grindstone in front of the door, a wok lay on the clay built open air stove. Master Wang said that this was Wangdaoling's kitchen and we would eat here. Blue cooking smoke became the scent of pines. The evening meal was noodles and Master Wang's potatoes.

After supper we went in to a great stone cave that resembled a large black wok. In the Ming dynasty the two hermits Wang Yao and Diao Ziran had lived here, hence its name, the Wangdiao Cave. Its walls were imprinted with the vestiges of smoke.

The cave had three chambers, the largest of 30 square meters. As you entered you left the light of day for the darkness of night. We felt our way to a bed and slept through to early the next morning. As we woke, outside the entrance to the cave the sun over the Zhongtiao Hills dyed the valley gold.

As ever, breakfast was Master Wang's noodles again. Afterwards he brought out a jar of herbal wine and offered me a bowl. After one bowlful I rapidly refused more. I was afraid that I would lie drunk in the cave and it would be a hundred years before I reached the bottom of the mountain.

The Maxian Cave was above the Wangdiao Cave at the top of a precipitous cliff but there was no clear path to it. When we had scrambled to the top we could only see the shallow traces left by the ancients. Fortunately there were iron chains

◀ Daoist master Wang cooking in the open air at Wangdaoling on Mount Huashan (Photo/Zhang Jianfeng)

to pull up by that indicated the way forward. During the Ming dynasty Ma Zhenyi had lived and practiced in the Wangdiao cave. A hundred years later in the Qing dynasty someone met him in northeastern China. Next to the Maxian cave I saw the "little square" that Master Li Mingji had spoken about. When they were practicing abstinence in the hills and did not leave the mountain for several months at a time, they sat in the little square when they were despondent and looked down the mountain towards the plains. They were at a height of more than 2,000 meters above sea level. Master Wang made his way up along a stone beam of no more than a hand's width to a stone hollow the size of a book, there was no way that he could sit there cross-legged so he sat with his feet dangling over the edge of the precipice. The wind came blowing in from the top of the cliff and I was anxious lest he should be blown over; my own legs were weakening and any thought of taking a few more photographs of Master Wang soon disappeared.

Master Wang said when he first arrived here he had survived for over 20 days on spring water and pine needles. Huashan recipe books dating back to ancient times mention pine needles, pine resin, mica, Solomon's seal, *lingzhi* fungus, poria mushrooms and knotweed. In a cave with pine trees growing at its mouth, Master Wang showed me the Solomon's seal they had prepared according to a secret recipe. This stuff, as black as stone, was their food. Only those hermits perched in the clouds knew the benefits of eating it.

Master Wang suggested that I should gather some pine needles to take down the mountain with me. He said that the best needles were those gathered during the dragon boat festival in June, on that day every plant became medicinal.

Sometimes the needles appeared in his teabowl. He said that it was possible to get drunk on tea and have a splitting headache afterwards. Anything could make you drunk, attachment to it was an obstacle but could also be a weapon.

I bowed farewell to Master Wang at the bottom of the mountain.

At a distance in time of several months and just as I was about to forget the Master Wang who lived on the upper reaches of the green river I revisited the mists of Mount Huashan. This time I first went to see Master Zou Tongxuan, the president of the Huashan Daoist Association and chairman of the Huashan Sect of the Complete Truth School of Daoism who lived at Cave Twenty. I said that I was investigating Daoism on Mount Huashan. He said that as he was familiar with the situation he could recommend several people to me.

At the Association I became acquainted with the overall situation of a number of practitioners: Master Shi lived at the Big Dipper Level and had given himself the title of Mountain Person of the Great Primordial (*taisu shanren*) and had lived as an ascetic for many years; the young Master Wen lived at Qingkeping and was interested in the bodily absorption of energy from the cosmos (*caiqi*), abstinence from cereals and the boiling of spring water for tea.

Having taken tea with President Zou I began my ascent to the Big Dipper Level. As I stepped through the stone entrance onto the level there were several workmen breaking up rock, perhaps it was undergoing a restoration, something difficult of achievement during the last hundred years. The building had been completely destroyed during the Cultural Revolution nearly fifty years ago, leaving just the stone cave. A daoist in patched clothing called to me to have a drink of water. He had been here more than 20 years, his surname was Shi and his title Mountain Person of the Great Primordial.

I had thought that the title *taisu*—the Great Primordial, had been borrowed from the name of a rock in the Huashan valley. The rock had been left over from the primal chaos of

211

antiquity. Primordial original energy is the essence of the energy that existed at the time before heaven and earth had become separate and it was believed that Mount Huashan itself was the primordial original energy.

Daoists believe that the cosmos of primordial matter that appeared before heaven and earth were split passed through five successive stages. These were the Great Change, the Great Start, the Great Beginning, the Great Primordial and the Great Ultimate or matrix of creation. The Great Primordial is one of the five stages before the transition of the Great Ultimate into the birth of heaven and earth. Liezi believed that the Great Primordial was the beginning of matter, the changing of the Great Beginning into form, once there was form then there was matter but not yet a state of *corpus*.

Master Shi said living here was a transition through a hundred years. Knowing that I had come because of my interest in the way, he said that it could not be spoken of lightly, our speech was already far removed from it. We could only talk about some of its residue.

He had met his teacher over twenty years ago. His teacher had been strange all his life, he spoke little and for many years he had hardly spoken with him at all. The first few years of his life as a daoist had almost been all work and there had been very little talking. Unless the time was ripe the master had not a word to say. There had been some people who had been with the master for some years and had left, only those with enough patience to stay were able to gain anything. At the end of their lives many people just had the merest something to pass on, perhaps just a few words. The way was not something to be casually handed out to people, passing it on to the wrong

◀ Daoist master Shi at the Big Dipper Level on Mount Huashan (Photo/Zhang Jianfeng)

person would incur the punishment of heaven.

When the workmen had finished in the courtyard, Master Shi took me to the top of the mountain to look at the clouds. The mist rose from the valley floor and followed the cliffs, swirling upwards towards the heavens. Hill dwellers called the mountain stairs to the clouds, and as the clouds rose, they climbed the mountain upwards. Without the mist things could be clearly made out, beauty and ugliness, high and low but when it was misty there was nothing. Mist and cloud came from heaven and returned to it. It came from and returned to the beginning.

I wanted to go to Dashangfang in the clouds across from Big Dipper Level, a place that ordinary people could not reach. Descending the mountain I passed Jiutiangong where Master Wang was in charge. Master Wen and Master Wang liked to practice. Master Wen spent most of the time in the Snow Flower Cave behind Jiutiangong, locked away for six months at a time without seeing anybody. On the previous occasion he had been unwilling to exchange more than a word with me, this time he was much more forthcoming. He said that every sentient being in the universe was an incarnation of the way, a tiny part of it that once separated could not return to its roots, the purpose of practicing the way was to enable a return to that original source. Once your own vital energy was at one with the way, you could control nature itself, command thunder and lightning and nurture every living thing. It was said that Master Wen was adept at magic but it was not something that he talked about.

Opposite Xiyixia I met daoist master Cheng who took care of the incense at the Cihang Temple. Master Cheng had not long left home for Daoism. He had wanted to study daoist medicine, heal the sick and promote Daoism. He said that he had been getting ready to practice Daoism for the last few years and that many years ago he had devised a way to be able to live in seclusion and practice Daoism. He had worked for ten years to earn money to give to his parents and had then gone up into the hills. He would spend the winter in this leaky stone hut. There was not much income from the sale of incense here and he had been obliged to accept some rice from the Daoist Association in order to get by. Life in the hills was tough but that was part of the process of practice. He was very willing to take me up to Dashangfang.

Wading across the river, the route up to Dashangfang was by way of a precipice several tens of meters high. Climbing with our faces against the cliff, we clambered through a cavern like a well before we had travelled even half the route. Dashangfang appeared as we were sitting in the clouds. It even had a vegetable patch, spring water and a mill-stone. President Cao wasn't on the mountain during this season and an elderly lay person was looking after the building.

Dashangfang is nearly 2,000 meters above sea level and there is a steep valley above. I wanted to find the Bowen Cave. But as the clouds covered us, the rain turned the surroundings into a small waterfall and we had to splash back through the rain. By the time we were back in the valley the mist and cloud had drifted to the top of the mountain in an act of soon to be accomplished sublimation.

The week before I planned to Mount Huashan I suddenly thought of telephoning daoist master Jingxiu (her Chinese name, her real name is Karine Martin). She had been born in Paris and nine years ago had come to the Southern Hills to pay homage to the great adept Ziyang, the compiler of the Song dynasty work on internal alchemy "Treatise on Awakening to Truth". She had then become a daoist nun in the Southern Hills. Previously she had taken a doctorate in medicine at the University of Paris.

When I telephoned she was in seclusion at Leigutai in the southern foothills of the Southern Hills. She said that she was just about to telephone me. During the nine years she had been in China she had always wanted to visit the Southern Hills.

Setting out from the southern suburbs of Xi'an, we missed the earliest train because of a traffic jam. The staff at the station changed our tickets to ones without seats and we squeezed onto the next train where we stood in the corridor next to the toilet.

I was beside the tap and she was between the toilet and the rubbish bin, she had to stand on tiptoe when people opened the door to the toilet and lift her hands when people dumped rubbish in the bin. The scene struck a chord in my memory and I was going to give her a nickname: Director of Toilets and Guardian of Rubbish but she forestalled me by saying: "Do you think I look like a fee collector?" We looked at each other and burst out laughing.

After standing for two hours we left the train at Mount Huashan station. After a bowl of noodles we went to a small hotel for a nap. Jingxiu took off her shoes and discovered that mice had chewed several small holes in them. She said that her father had taken her to buy these shoes when she had left home. They were a pair of the best French shoes and had cost about 1,000 yuan ten years ago. They had accompanied her all over the world and it was hard to imagine that they would take their last step on Mount Huashan. To ease her grief I said that as her shoes had died she should give them a grave and put up a headstone.

We went first to the Yuquan Temple to pay our respects to the statue of Hao Datong the founder of the Huashan School where the daoist master in charge recognized Jingxiu. President Zou of the Daoist Association was away and we lost the opportunity of free entrance to the mountain. In my eyes the principal peak of Mount Huashan stood like a piece of jade, pure and unblemished against the clear sky, gentle and unstained by the dust of the world. On a rock at the side of the path were inscribed the characters "Mountain of Longevity" (*shou shan*) in the hand of the great ancestor of Daoism, Chen Tuan. Perhaps it was here, facing the mountain, that he had been unable to conceal his joy.

Jingxiu and I planned to stay first at Jiutiangong where there was spring water for tea and comfortable beds. Under the August sun, mist rose everywhere and I felt the energy from my body floating heavenwards as transparent heat. My clothes were soon soaked in sweat but it was a matter for congratulation that there were many fewer mosquitoes on Mount Huashan than in the Southern Hills. Nevertheless, there were several that were soon attracted by the odor of sweat. Being bitten was as painful as an injection and left a blister. Although I tried to be merciful and let them take a drink, they were too greedy and I soon carelessly broke the commandment against killing. They seemed to have even more interest in Jingxiu, perhaps they believed that her Parisian blood was perfumed.

Perhaps it was because the weather was so hot but the sound of the river was quieter. In places the riverbed had appeared, in other places the water had disappeared underground and made its way weakly forward by a circuitous route.

It was nearly dark by the time that we reached Jiutiangong. Master Wen was waiting for us in his tea house while taking the opportunity to practice his calligraphy. Since I had last left the mountain Master Wen had spent six months in one of the valleys of the Southern Hills. He had found a place for solitary practice where it was said that neither the sound of birds nor women could be heard. There were those who said that he was undertaking some sort of secret practice.

He had returned here some months ago. He was younger

217

than before, so much so that there appeared to be something child-like about him. Night and day he spent almost all his time meditating in the cave behind the temple. To use his own words, he had no interest in anything else apart from practice.

Master Wen produced all the good tea that the temple had stored away including some fine Wulong tea presented by a lay person from Taiwan. After drinking tea I took the pot to the valley to fetch water. The water on Mount Huashan is always a blue-green and whether it is rushing down the valley or still the color never changes.

The color is even more beautiful when the water is with tea in a bowl.

I drank tea every time I came to Jiutiangong. The drinking of tea and the practice of Daoism were the characteristic of the place. With the soft tea gurgling in my throat I recalled this season the previous year when Master Wen had taken me up the rocks behind the temple to pick akebia fruit. They only hung from trees by the cliff and rather resembled kiwi fruit. In August their skins split and when peeled the fruit looked like the snow in October. The flesh contained evenly distributed black seeds and it tasted like a banana but cool and sweet. I liked the flavor which made me think of the taste of snow in the winter when I was small, cool with a hint of sweetness.

When it was dark Master Wen bid us goodnight and went back to his cave. I stood in the courtyard and began to practice the rhythmic breathing that he had taught me last time. Practice over, I ate the snow white noodles prepared by practitioner Liu and then went straight to sleep.

Early next morning I woke Jingxiu and we set off into the valley. We first had to go into the valley and then climb up opposite the river at the Suoluo Level to Dashangfang at the top of Mount Baiyun.

As we sat resting on a shoulder of the mountain, Jingxiu

discovered that her hairpin was missing. I joked that she was an imitation daoist. Just then the mountain breeze lifted her hair, Jingxiu smiled in relief and said: "Look, isn't the mountain breeze the best hairpin of all?"

We soon started to climb the route to Dashangfang but it was harder than the previous time and not such a thrill as before.

We rested twice on the way and arrived at the cave where the god of thunder had his home. More precisely it was a ravine with the thunder god sitting where it was slightly broader. There was a precipice in front of the god and by the top of his head was a tunnel like a well with steps and hand-chains leading upwards. Above it was Dashangfang.

I discovered by accident that there was even a cable at the side of the path. It looked as if there was electricity at the top of the mountain.

Previously, the main construction on Dashangfang had been the cave in the cliff-face. There was now a daoist temple formed from the cave and a stone building called the Temple of the Perfected Warrior (*Zhenwu*). In the universe, the Grand Emperor Zhenwu controls the heaven and earth of the North as well as warfare world-wide.

We met a daoist nun at the entrance to the temple. She greeted us hurriedly, took us to the door of Master Cao's room and then rushed into the kitchen.

Master Cao's room was minute. Fortunately I was the right size, had I been any fatter I would never have got through the door. Master Cao was sitting cross-legged on the *kang* reading the classics. The room was so small that it was almost impossible to stand upright. I sat down beside the *kang* but Jingxiu immediately reminded me that I should stand, Master Cao was a female daoist and I should keep my distance.

Master Cao looked full of energy and seemed unfazed by

our arrival. She was 84 and was one of the few female daoist masters. She had come with her mother to Mount Huashan over 60 years earlier to become a daoist. Her teacher, Master Mei Jiarui had put her in the Ziqitai Temple below Nantianmen. From 1959 on, many daoists had been forced off the mountain to join production brigades. In order to continue practicing she had hidden in a pit in the depths of Mount Taibai for 12 years until a change in religious policy restored the freedom to choose a life of practice. She had then returned to Mount Huashan and continued to practice.

I sought her instructions on where one would start in practice, she said straight away: "Learn how to conduct oneself," and lowering her head continued to read.

I asked further: "One can behave well off the mountain, what is so different on the mountain?"

She replied: "It's a bit more tranquil."

In order to break the silence I carried on and asked: "It requires a lifetime of application to become a good person but once completed life is over as well, does this mean that the practice of the way is also complete?"

She muttered under her breath for a moment, looked at me and said: "Of course not, you think only of behavior, once completed the founding father will naturally come and make you an immortal."

When it was time to eat, an elderly lay person brought some vegetarian food: dates and peanuts and told us that Master Cao's diet for the last few years had included no cereals and only herbs, peanuts, potatoes and dates.

As we were resting under the eaves drinking tea after having seen Master Cao, I saw two other nuns. This exceeded my imagination. Dashangfang had never been so busy. One of

▶ Daoist master Cao at Dashangfang on Mount Huashan (Photo / Zhang Jianfeng)

the nuns wore a white daoist gown and as she walked seemed about to fly away.

She wore a piece of jade at the back of her head. It was only when I greeted her that I realized that she had brought her disciple—an even younger nun—with her to Dashangfang from the mountains of Sichuan. I wanted to know her daoist title and inadvertently disclosed my own identity. She had come across a copy of *Seeking the Way* which I edited when staying at the buddhist college at Mount Jiuhuashan, as well as some of the hermits that I had written about. She did not want to be a subject for my pen and so refused to tell me her title. I secretly gave her a title: Master Qingfeng (Pure Wind) and her disciple was Mingyue (Bright Moon).

Master Cao was Master Qingfeng's teacher and she said that they were here to cadge some food off her, bursting into laughter as she spoke.

Food supplies for Dashangfang were provided by the Huashan Daoist Association at the Yuquan Temple, but only to Master Cao who then distributed rations to the others. No vegetables had been sent up for a long time and we just had potatoes for lunch. The old lay person brought us a bowlful and we sat in the shade of a tree in the courtyard peeling potatoes.

Leaning against the stone wall I dozed in the blue kitchen smoke. After I woke I hauled myself up the iron chains to a small cave which had been chiseled from the rock on a precipice about 100 meters above ground. Once you were in there was just room for a few things but if you lay down you had to curl up in order to fit. I sat cross-legged and looking out, could see the western peak of Mount Huashan and the pines of Luoyanfeng. The field of view was vast and the scenery wonderful but I was afraid that if I stayed any longer I would become giddy and fall.

Once back on the ground lunch was ready. Without

standing on ceremony Jingxiu and I joined the ranks of the diners. For many days afterwards the taste of those golden potatoes stubbornly stayed with me and they appeared often in my dreams.

After lunch Master Qingfeng nimbly climbed the roof like a martial arts hero in a film and as Mingyue handed her the tools she filled the chinks between the roof and the tiles with mud. Master Cao lit incense before each of the statues, including the kitchen god and the earth god and then returned to the *kang* to continue reciting.

I looked towards the Temple of the Perfected Warrior as I stood opposite and inwardly said a prayer for Master Qingfeng beneath whose feet the boundless abyss was as deep as the sky itself. The rooms of the temple were built on the edge of a precipice, everything swayed in the wind and the ancient wooden door blew open and shut with the wind. In order to prevent them being blown away the towels on the forks of the tree were knotted. The plants in the courtyard unfolded in the wind and black seeds rustled down, a new life had started a different journey.

I lay sprawled on the steps in front of the temple and watched some ants moving house until the stars glowed orange in the sky like so many flowers.

As darkness fell Master Qingfeng at last returned to the ground. After she had washed her hands she called to us and said that she would take us to an interesting place. Jingxiu and I followed close behind. Her every movement seemed to be a rallying cry and I think I would not have refused even if she had led us straight up a precipice. However, she took us climbing to the top of a large rock that stood high over Master Cao's hut.

Master Qingfeng stood on the summit of the rock and hauled Jingxiu to the top as if she were a pillow. I scrambled up as well and saw not a precipice but a sky full of stars and the lights on the hill opposite.

She said that they had once been like me and wandered all over the mountains of the Southern Hills and had spent about a year on Mount Taibai.

I lay on the rock and listened to Master Mingyue telling her story.

She said, do you know the scent of the lotus flower? On summer evenings we put the tea leaves that we have picked on the stamen of the lotus flower and during the night the bud closes. Early next morning the petals open and we collect the tea leaves from the flower and soak them in spring water. They have absorbed the fragrance of the lotus flower. We collect the fragrance of all sorts of flowers this way.

Master Mingyue's voice sounded like silver and put me in mind of a skylark on a spring bough. Of all the places that she had visited she thought that Mount Taibai was the most beautiful, the clouds were whiter and the weather attractively cold. In the winter your hand would stick to the towel when you went to pick it up after washing your face. The trees were tall and at night you could lie there as they swayed in the wind and through the gaps you could gaze at the distant sky while you waited for the moon to rise.

Night hung over all and amidst the coldly shining hills there was only my own shadow and the moonlight. In this kind of solitude you can sense the miracle of life. In the hills the moon is larger than it is off the mountain. I often fell asleep in a tree while watching the moon and was woken by the wind, sometimes at dawn.

As I listened to Master Qingfeng, I too felt that I was asleep in the moonlight under the night sky and that opening my eyes I could see the richest starlit sky in the world. The stars filled the sky like wild chrysanthemums flowering in the autumn

▲ Looking at the stars from Dashangfang with masters Qingfeng and Mingyue (Photo/Zhang Jianfeng)

countryside. They blossomed for those who appreciated them. My eyes greedily drank them in as my ears took in the sound of the wind in the mountains.

Master Mingyue said that in all these years their feet had never rested, they had always been on the go, in the wind, rain and snow, at night and during the day. When others had been celebrating New Year they had still been on the move.

At times one had wanted an answer, why was it like this? Now, however, the answer was unimportant, movement had its own delights. They often encountered a white bearded old practitioner of nearly a hundred who also wandered abroad. If they did not meet him here they would meet him somewhere else. Li Bai, the Tang poet was the same, he spent a lifetime wandering the hills and rivers.

She had accompanied her teacher to many mountains,

though, in fact, the more you travelled the lighter it seemed. Apart from study there was not much work here with her teacher's master, either they climbed the hills or slept on the rocks. Every morning her teacher's master rose earlier than the squirrels in the trees and coughed several times outside Master Mingyue's window. If, after a while, there was no response, she would call her pupil Qingfeng's name and say: "Go and see if that lazy cat is still asleep." When she heard this Mingyue would rush to open the door and accompany her teacher and her teacher's master to the cave to recite the classics.

Her teacher's master's food included dates which Mingyue was very fond of. When her teacher's master was eating Mingyue would gaze unblinkingly at the food and the master would stare at her in a war of looks.

Later the master would smile and say: "Greedy cat" and Mingyue would receive some of the food from the master's bowl. Finally Mingyue would make her case by saying: "Master, if you don't eat up your food the rats will get it, rather than make a present of it to the rats, why not bestow some of it upon the 'greedy cat'?" Master Cao laughed like a child and said: "I'm at fault! I'm at fault!"

That night I was installed in my sleeping quarters, a ground floor storeroom with a *kang*. I had just stepped through the door when a rat loudly greeted its new fellow lodger. I heard the sound with long suffering and excitement.

The *kang* was very large and I only occupied part of it and I thought that my fluffy friends could dance on its broad surface if they wanted.

Early next morning Master Qingfeng planned to go down the mountain and return with a sack of vegetables. By the time that I was standing above the Temple of the Perfected Warrior ready to take some photographs Master Cao had already finished chanting and was weeding in the vegetable patch and so I went to join her.

The cabbages growing in the patch were not yet ready for the kitchen. Master Cao gathered some wild spinach from outside the vegetable patch which later appeared on the breakfast table. Breakfast started after Master Cao had lit incense in front of all the statues of gods and of the kitchen god as well. The meal consisted of porridge, *mantou* and potatoes.

After breakfast I shouldered my rucksack ready to go down the mountain and Jingxiu went to say goodbye to Master Cao. She had told me mysteriously that she wanted to have her as her teacher. Before I could respond she had already gone into Master Cao's room. Master Cao's attitude to this French practitioner was one of uninhibited affection and she accepted her request.

I tried to find an opportunity to suggest to Jingxiu that she should quickly say goodbye to Master Cao but Master Cao got out of the way and made Jingxiu perform an obeisance to the statue of Guanyin in the refectory. Afterwards Master Cao wrote out a new daoist title for her on a sheet of paper: Jingzongxiu. Before this Jingxiu had been a disciple of the 32nd generation of the Longmen sect of the daoist school of Complete Truth, she had now become a disciple of the 23rd generation.

It took us about an hour to get down from Dashangfang and back to the Suoluo Level. After a short rest we carried on up the mountain. We reached Qingkeping just as Jingzongxiu's strength was about to give out.

Two days of trekking about had worn out her heels and I guessed that she would not be able to continue.

Back at Jiutiangong Master Wen produced a pile of tea leaves and welcomed us as generously as ever. After supper two foreigners arrive in search of accommodation and began to chat with Jingzongxiu. She came in a little later to say that she couldn't accompany me anymore and that she would return to Xi'an the next day with her two French compatriots.

They both spoke good Chinese and had come to China in search of the way and to work. Drawn by the hermits and the practice of Daoism, they had wanted to visit the Southern Hills. Jingzongxiu took out her telephone, my name had been replaced by the English word "Hermits". She told them that if they were looking for hermits they could come to me for help. She also told them that I had a map with me that was used for looking for hermits. They fell for it and immediately crowded round and asked me to write down on a piece of paper the names of those hermits who would not object to being sought out.

It rained all night and next morning, planning to cross the ridge in search of the hermit in Xianyu that Master Wen had mentioned, I shouldered my pack and said goodbye to Jingzongxiu and Master Wen. As I was going out of the door, Master Wen picked two cucumbers from the vegetable patch for me to eat on the way. Unable to refuse I took one and then started the climb up behind Jiutiangong, the steepest part of the route.

On the way I thought of the hermit that Master Wen said lived in the depths of Xianyu. It was said that everyone who had met him had been attracted by the sound of his *qin*. He carried the *qin* on his back wherever he went and even slept with it by his side.

According to Master Wen' directions I needed to wade across the river and would find the hermit's hut on the river bank. I imagined him sitting by the river, with mist rising from the water, the sound of the *qin* making rings of vapor in the air and rolling past the blue-green rocks and the dark green moss.

At the top of the ridge, sunlight filled the whole valley. The ridge was like a market with the space totally occupied by tourists and the stalls of souvenir sellers.

Dark clouds were moving across the hills to the south as I went downhill along the ridge of Lianhuafeng (Lotus flower Peak). Looking north I thought I could see the Yellow River and the Wei River but in front of me it was just white mist. I started to walk towards the area forbidden to tourists. Behind me stood tall peaks, alternately green and white, that seemed to have grown from ink and were hidden vaguely in the mist. A path stretched out behind the Tourist Bureau employees' hostel towards the upper reaches of the river.

After the start of the rainy season, the mountains became a world of grass. The orchid-like grass beside the path and fresh green covered the whole path like a basket. I met somebody behind the hostel and asked him about the place where the hermit was. He said that there was only a family of hill dwellers there, it was probably about two hours walk, my mind was firm.

He suggested that I needed a walking stick to warn the snakes in the grass to get out of the way. I did as he suggested and a length of tree root washed down by the river became the staff which I used to separate the waist-high grass.

There were some huts by the river with padlocked doors. Some herbs were drying on a rock by the river and the herb gatherer's carrying pole was still there. There was no trace of anybody around. There were a few peach trees by the river and the fur of the peaches on them had not yet split. Sometimes the path was just a few rocks in the river and it was almost impossible to see where human hand had placed them so that one proceeded by instinct. After about an hour I discovered that I had lost my way.

The river bed became wider and wider with huge rocks everywhere and no sign of bird or beast. Apart from rocks it was all tree-like grass, take half a step in and you were submerged. There was nobody from whom to enquire the way, just the black tadpoles swimming to and fro in the water. I could only retrace my steps and eventually found traces of the path in the grass.

I scooped up a mouthful of water and drank my fill. The water struck the inside of my mouth with the rawness of alcohol, though on second tasting it was weak and flavorless. When I turned round I noticed a pair of straw sandals on a rock but didn't see either a herb gatherer or a herdsman, may be the sandals belonged to the river god. If the river god wore no sandals perhaps the river would flood.

I looked up and saw thick cloud in the depths of the valley. I broke into a trot and eventually found several piles of animal dung at the bottom of a cliff. This encouraged me. My destination could not be far off. Finally, I discovered three oxen in a wood who immediately made way for this unwelcome guest.

Hoof prints began to appear all over the beach of the river but as ever there were no people. I thought there might be a straw hut nearby and looking round the valley spotted several flags and a hut under a cave-like cliff. The hut was built under the cliff-face and the path up the cliff had been trodden into a myriad tracks by the oxen. Afraid of disturbing the tranquility of the hermit I suppressed the temptation to rush in shouting. I thought he might be sitting there in meditation waiting for me.

Reaching the entrance to the hut in a single breath I couldn't help laughing. It was the shed for the oxen, filled with their smell. The door was open and red, yellow and green flags fluttered in the breeze. I immediately thought of the three oxen, the three flags must be something they enjoyed, set there to remind them not to be mesmerized by the sight of green grass and forget the way home.

I followed the stream down from the cowshed and finally

caught sight of several huts at the confluence of two rivers. I hopped across the rocks to the opposite bank and a dog appeared in front of me to be immediately followed by an even larger one that rushed at me barking furiously.

I have no good impression of dogs, their arrival made me feel a robber substitute or at the very least *persona non grata*. I guessed that they might bite me somewhere on the leg. As they rushed past I suddenly remembered that I still had a piece of moldy biscuit in my pack.

I had picked up the biscuit from beside a shop on the mountain, planning to make a midday meal of it on the way. I now broke it in two and threw it, the dogs seized the pieces at once and I seized the opportunity to make my way to the huts.

Once they had eaten the biscuit, the dogs blocked my path once more. They threatened me until they had eaten the remaining biscuit in my hand. At this point the door of the hut opened and a pipe-smoking hill dweller appeared. He seemed to have timed his appearance just at the right moment. The two dogs started to wag their tails at me.

I asked the old man whether the *qin* playing hermit lived hereabouts. He said he didn't know.

I thought perhaps that he may not have understood what I said and repeated it in dialect. The reply was still that he didn't know.

I sat down on a stone in the courtyard and opened my pack to see if I had a packet of cigarettes I could give him. I turned out the whole pack but had to apologize and say that I had brought no cigarettes with me. Perhaps because of my sincerity, he suddenly said, is that the hermit you are looking for? He lives in the hut across the river.

I looked back and saw that there was a hut beside the river. The hill dweller suggested that I should share enjoyment of the pipe with him but I declined. If I had not given up smoking

I would certainly have taken several fierce puffs.

Across the river and back on the path I started to run and saw in the distance a lean daoist priest standing by the side of the path. I thought that he should have a long beard but I didn't see one. He said that he had been sitting in his hut when I passed and had called to me. Unfortunately I hadn't heard and consequently had given the biscuit to the two dogs.

I followed behind him through plantain and wild flowers whose name I did not know to a hut on the river bank. The grass in front of the door was luxuriant and it was impossible to detect any sign of human movement. This was why I had overlooked the hut. I had thought it was abandoned.

Inside the hut it was like a cave. The daoist filled a basin of rice gruel and handed me a bowl of paprika. He said that apart from this there were no other vegetables that he could serve. This was what he ate

▲ Siguo Cliff on Mount Huashan (Photo/Zhang Jianfeng)

every day.

I remembered that I still had the cucumber the Master Wen had given me in my pack and produced it. The master said that it would go well with my rice. I suggested that he should keep it, we went backwards and forwards and eventually I left it on the hearth.

I looked at the paprika and looked at the green grass by the door, swallowed and quickly drank all the rice gruel.

The daoist master said that he had been drinking the rice gruel for two days already. In the winter he cooked a basin of gruel and it lasted three days. In the summer it lasted two days. When he felt like vegetables he stir-fried some Solomon's seal. One batch of cooking would last for a long time.

I suggested that he should play a tune on the *qin*. He said that had forgotten it. It was all a long time ago. He had given away the *qin* when he had come to the mountains. There was no need for surplus belongings here. I found no tea in the hut and just had to drink water. I sat on a tree stump and watched the waves of wind in the pine trees and, lost in thought, listened to the sound of the water.

The master went out for a walk in the middle of the day. There was a *kang* beneath the window through which the mountain peaks could be seen. The presence of this window triggered the return of my old habit of fantasizing. I imagined a small moon in a vast night-sky and outside the window neither past nor present just the solitary river and the wind plucking at one's clothes.

I woke from this noon nap to the sound of running water, there was no sign of the master and the mountain rain had started to fall sounding like surf on a beach. In a little while the sun came out. I stood on a rock by the river and picked some walnuts. I smashed the shells with a stone, peeled away the green skin and extracted the sweet tasting kernel to assuage the loneliness of my stomach.

The master returned from his walk as darkness approached. He said that sometimes he went for a walk and walked at random in the mountain wilds. If he took the fork in the valley path, half a day's walk would bring him to Wangdaoling, the other way would bring him to the foothills of the Southern Hills.

I asked what was to be gained from living here?

He said that there was nothing to be gained. Had he sought gain he would not have come to the hills. Here one could comprehend the way. The way was beyond the world and not governed by the worldly norms of good and evil. Animals were basically predatory, however they could be trained quite easily, but according to your standards not those of nature. There are many wolves on the plains of the north and they often eat the herdsmen's sheep. Some years ago hunters took to shooting the wolves and soon eradicated them only to discover that the sheep then died in large numbers from disease. Wolves were subsequently imported from elsewhere and the flocks of sheep began to revive.

Life and death are natural, heaven grants life and heaven brings death. That is a principle of the way. If all that you can see is man then you can only speak and take decisions on the basis of the human way; if your vision can encompass the whole world then you can go beyond man and other life and the great way is the whole universe itself.

Mankind attempts to solve its ills, but in fact there are ills which do not require a solution, merely toleration. If you take clouds for example, in an instant they seem to grow and obscure the sun and moon, but in fact it is only your vision that is obscured. If your eyes can see the limitless space then the rest can be ignored. What is there that may not be tolerated? In my eyes, the *qin* was the whole world, once I got rid of it I saw a larger world. It is man that has ills and man that needs to purify himself.

The valley grew darker and in the blink of an eye the mist descended over the eaves of the hut and it began to rain.

I very much wanted to stay but I was alas in two minds. There were matters in town that tugged at me and I could not cut them away.

The daoist detected my dilemma and said that I should hurry on down the mountain. If I left it too late I would be caught by heavy rain and if the river rose I would be in trouble. He then found me a raincoat.

With my rucksack on my back I hurriedly said goodbye and trotted along the river bed with the rain urging me on from behind.

The rain caught up with me at the place where the oxen had been and the raincoat appeared utterly useless. The wind blew it aside and I was completely soaked. Very soon I was unable to open my eyes and the rain poured down my face like a waterfall. My shoes filled with water when I crossed the river.

Speed fell victim to the rain and I just trudged slowly on. At the entrance to the valley I picked some peaches by the pathway and tucked them away as I went on down the mountain.

The rain was illuminated by sunlight as I emerged from the valley and after the rain stopped the mountains appeared like a gleaming dewdrop.

I suppressed the urge to collect up these pearls of water and take them back to town. They could clear the eyes of many so that they could see through the dust of the city to the blue of the hills as they rose and fell into the distance towards the horizon where crystal waters flowed, wild flowers swayed in the wind and white clouds floated at ease.

Postscript

Dye Garments to the White of Clouds, Forget the Day of Return

The Southern Hills had been waiting for me for a myriad years and I wandered through the dust of the world and eventually reached them.

— For years I lived in a city at the foot of the hills without realizing that this was an extraordinary mountain until the day we looked out and became aware of its beauty.

Over the last few years, the self that is me, has spent most of the time walking the Southern Hills as if, somewhere in the depths of cloud there were several ancients awaiting me.

Before I started on my journey I had a very long dream about searching for hermits in the hills. At the moment I can't really decide whether my journey was an even longer dream. For most of the time the hermits were unwilling to be disturbed, the deeper they hid themselves the more I wanted to find them, as if we were playing a game of hide-and-seek.

For the most part our attitude is one of investigative voyeurism and not of concern for their existence. They are the familiar faces of the past who because they seek something more from life have left the crowd to seek solitude.

I encountered danger a number of times in the hills: snakes, falls, losing the way, but these dangers and difficulties evaporated in the face of the hermits. What they cast away we take up. Many years ago a figure walked the road towards the Southern Hills in search of the hermits. Bill Porter, the bearded American, came to these hills 20 years earlier than I and recorded his love and admiration for the Southern Hills and its inhabitants. Today, in the lamplight, people still read his descriptions of the hermits of the Southern Hills of the *Road to Heaven*, just as I dreamed that first dream of hermits.

In a valley of the Southern Hill I met a pair of "Immortal Companions", he had lived in the valley with his girlfriend for eight years. He loved the white clouds, the flow of water and the air. Life in the hills had brought him contentment and for most of the time he studied, played the *qin*, painted, gathered herbs and tilled the soil.

Apart from practice, people in the hills love life more than we do. When they meet outsiders some hide but more hurry to prepare them a meal. In the hills I felt I had returned home. My mother was like that every time I went home hurrying to prepare a meal in case I was hungry. If you are hungry in the hills, they will bring you a bowl of rice, absolutely without thinking of the money in your pocket.

Perhaps they understand life better and we just corral ourselves. I learned about life from them. They do not place themselves outside life. It is just that they have already abandoned the material things that we seek.

I had always thought that hermits ignored life but it is the exact opposite. They cherish certain abilities and an ideal harmonious lifestyle.

In the Southern Hills nothing separates man and animals and there are no misunderstandings. They are all neighbors.

When I put down my pen and look back on the search for the hermits of the Southern Hills, two years seem to have slipped away. Nanshan Sanren and his companion have moved even deeper into the hills, some of the hermits on the rear slope of Mount Huashan have left the mountain, Master Tan has disappeared without trace and some hermits have left this world. Nevertheless, more and more people are living in seclusion in the Southern Hills. Together with a number of friends of the way I am building a meeting place for hermits which is now taking shape and will accommodate some ten people at a time. More huts and cottages have appeared in the Southern Hills and media reports suggest the presence of some 5,000 hermits. The hermits of the Southern Hills have caused an unprecedented sensation in China.

I was always looking for the Southern Hills in the Southern Hills. The ultimate South lies in every peak of the Southern Hills, there is no fixed point that is the Southern Hills and I believe that beyond the Southern Hills that I can see, there is another Southern Hills that I cannot.